Also by Tom Piazza

My Cold War: A Novel
Blues and Trouble: Twelve Stories
The Guide to Classic Recorded Jazz
True Adventures with the King of Bluegrass
Blues Up and Down
Setting the Tempo (editor)

Also by Wynton Marsalis

To a Young Jazz Musician (with Selwyn Seyfu Hinds)
Jazz in the Bittersweet Blues of Life (with Carl Vigeland)
Marsalis on Music
Sweet Swing Blues on the Road (with Frank Stewart)
Jazz for Young People™ Curriculum
Foreword to *The NPR Curious Listener's Guide to Jazz*
    (by Loren Schoenberg)
Ballads
Standards: Trumpet Transcriptions
    with Piano Score

Also by Jazz at Lincoln Center Education

Jazz for Young People™ Curriculum
The Student Musician's Guide to Jazz

Understanding

JAZZ

Tom Piazza

Produced by
Jazz at Lincoln Center

Foreword by Wynton Marsalis

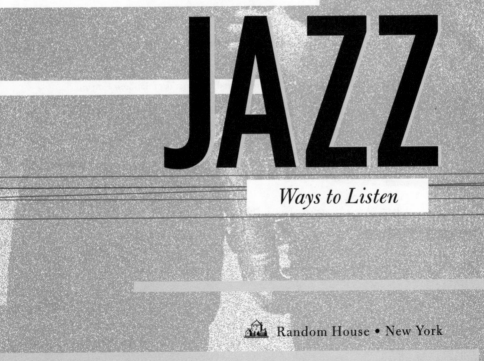

Understanding

JAZZ

Ways to Listen

Random House • New York

Dizzy Gillespie and Sonny Stitt, 1953.
Photograph by Herman Leonard Photography, LLC.

Published in the United States by Random House, an imprint of The Random House Publishing Group, a division of Random House, Inc., New York.

RANDOM HOUSE and colophon are registered trademarks of Random House, Inc.

LIBRARY OF CONGRESS CATALOGING-IN-PUBLICATION DATA

Piazza, Tom
Understanding jazz: ways to listen / Tom Piazza.
p. cm.
ISBN 1-4000-6369-8
I. Jazz—Analysis, appreciation. I. Title.
MT146.P53 2005
781.65'117—dc22   2005046569

Printed in the United States of America on acid-free paper

www.atrandom.com

987654321

First Edition

Book design by Mercedes Everett

Foreword
Wynton Marsalis

I come from a family of musicians. We all grew up listening to jazz in one form or another. That's not to say we liked it. We particularly disliked attending live concerts. No light shows, no dancing girls, no lyrics . . . just people—old people—playing instruments for what seemed like forever. Somehow, though, most of our family developed the ability to hear the meaning in jazz. For me, this happened at age twelve while listening to John Coltrane's "Cousin Mary." Suddenly, I could understand what the musicians were saying. It was like breaking some impenetrable code; valuable secrets were revealed.

Now, my younger brother Ellis couldn't understand all this fuss about jazz. He wasn't a musician, and jazz just didn't speak to him. He had his own favorite pop groups whose songs accompanied the special periods and events in his life—tunes that still evoke the feeling of those times. For Ellis, the distance between those short vocal songs with the drums slapping on beats two and four and an eight-minute saxophone solo with the drums playing all wild, a walking bass, and *no words* . . . whew, that was too long a distance to travel! In spite of all that, one day he heard a relationship between a Michael Jackson song (that he really liked) and a Louis Armstrong piece that he remembered from the deep past of childhood. He figured it might be worth it to learn to hear jazz. Some years later, when we had moved away from home, he called me and said, "Man, I think I hear it. I can hear what y'all are playing."

I knew exactly what *it* he was talking about. This hearing of *it* is the moment of revelation that leads you deeper into a love of jazz. All at once, the potential glories of interacting with this limitless music become evident and present, *pressing*. All the head-scratching and confusion are replaced with excitement and expectation. You are welcomed into a club that never dwindles— the *It* club.

When you ride a bike for the first time, or drive a car on a freeway without panic, or learn how to be quiet when your mother tells you something you really don't like, you understand the *it* of those things. You see, everything has an *it* to it. You're never too old to experience *it*, and once you get *it*, you never lose *it*.

Membership in the *It* club of jazz listeners doesn't require a secret handshake or a poetic nickname. After all, hearing jazz is not that difficult. *Following* jazz is where all the trouble begins. But when you begin to think of jazz in terms of language, you'll see how much you already know. We're all improvisers when we speak, making things up as we go along, using the base of our experience, education, and knowledge to communicate effectively.

Jazz musicians improvise the same way. We try to express ourselves clearly, drawing on a mental database of melodies, rhythms, and textures. All of us, however, are experts in the musical manipulation of words. Subtle changes in pitch, inflection, rhythm, and timbre give our sentences completely different meanings; one more high-pitched *pleeeeease* and you'll get your peanut butter and jelly sandwich. Jazz musicians will bend a note here or repeat a phrase there to create the desired effect. And that's what we love to do.

Consider how easy it is to identify someone's speaking voice—just listen to the tone and rhythm of his or her speech. Go a level deeper, and you begin to identify the ideology, how he or she combines ideas and beliefs to construct a way of being. The same applies to the sounds and styles of a jazz musician. Thelonious Monk's piano sounds different from Keith Jarrett's, and it doesn't take long to hear this. Listen a little closer and you'll be able to identify the similarities and differences in their musical philosophies. You'll begin to notice the temperament of certain musicians—the cool of Lester Young, the wit of Clark Terry, the tenderness of Ben Webster, the power of Art Blakey, and so many more. That's why we say jazz is a language—a language of words, beyond words.

Also, in speaking musically, there is the overall spirit in the sound of a voice. And if we think about it, the most successful speakers communicate essences that go far beyond the power of words or ideology. There's an *it* in the sound. Some call it charisma, some call it sanctified, some call it magic. Regardless, when we hear *it*, we love it. Much of the meaning in Dr. Martin Luther King's speeches lies in the magic of his sound. And much of the meaning in jazz reverberates in the charismatic sounds of its great musicians. That's why it's essential for a musician to speak in his or her own voice. When you can identify the spirit of these powerful voices, the *sound* enriches your soul.

As musicians, we do our best to share *it* with our audiences in each performance. If everyone's swinging, that *it* takes over. Time and time again and around the globe, I've found that when an audience really gets *it*, a room can rise right up off the ground. When playing for an audience of enthusiastic *It* club members, jazz musicians discover even more to share—more of *it*. *It* becomes the most precious of gifts, growing as it's given, like love.

I hope that *Understanding Jazz* uncovers the many wondrous personalities of jazz and reveals the process of making first-rate jazz music. This music can provide energy, affirmation, and enlightenment. Most of all, though, I hope that *Understanding Jazz* helps you tap in to your inner ear, the sense that illuminates the music of everyday details that so often go unheard. *It*, after all, is all around us.

In the spirit of swing,

Wynton Marsalis
Artistic Director,
Jazz at Lincoln Center

P.S. I know you have a lot of listening ahead of you (the seven tracks on the companion CD are just the beginning), but don't forget to check out *Thelonious Monk: Live at the It Club—Complete*, released by Legacy in 1982. And when the *It* club reconvenes, we have to work on that secret handshake.

Contents

Introduction

Jazz music is about one hundred years old as of this writing, and those hundred years have been a long and winding road indeed. Born out of a crazy quilt of cultural influences in the early years of the twentieth century, mainly in New Orleans, jazz has since spread around the world and profoundly influenced virtually every form of Western music.

Despite its history and wide influence, jazz music has been more appreciated than understood, both by the general public and by the academic music establishment. Partly this is because jazz is a hybrid form—part popular art, part fine art. It is hard to categorize and define simply. How can a music be improvised and "serious" at the same time? How can it have a form and yet be different in every performance? How can performers who place so much emphasis on individuality and spontaneity put themselves at the service of a coherent group sound? These questions, and others like them, have tended to make jazz a bit of a puzzle, at least from the outside.

This book attempts to answer these questions. It is not a history of jazz. It doesn't contain biographical material about its great practitioners, or a chronological survey of the development of styles, or a comprehensive guide to recorded jazz. It is instead a guide to getting oriented in a jazz performance, a look into the mind, in a sense, of a jazz group. It consists of a set of six separate but intimately related explorations into the nature of jazz, and it is designed to help you learn to recognize landmarks, to hear how the parts relate to the whole.

At the beginning of the marvelous book *Aspects of the Novel,* E. M. Forster invites his readers to imagine themselves in a room where all the novelists in the history of literature, without regard to chronology or stylistic division, are writing together. Ideally, I would ask something of the same sort. The present book is concerned more with elements that can be found and discussed in jazz regardless of era or style. The pianist and composer Mary Lou Williams—whose experience stretched from playing with territory bands in the 1920s in the Midwest to performing with Cecil Taylor, the most avant of the avant-garde, in the 1970s, and who was also a great supporter of the bebop players of the 1940s—was fond of saying, "All eras in the history of jazz were modern."

Understanding Jazz is not meant to be a definitive résumé of the possibilities in jazz. It is rather a series of avenues into understanding the music. While discussed separately, these avenues are interdependent, like the members of a jazz group. The separations are, in a sense, artificial, intended to focus the eye on an aspect of what should finally be understood as a total, integrated picture.

Jazz has had many incarnations and many guises. Aficionados speak of New Orleans jazz, of Kansas City jazz, of cool jazz and bebop, of West Coast jazz and avant-garde. Yet all these different approaches, and more, these dialects, have important things in common, family resemblances. Jazz mixes great musical sophistication with a vitalizing earthiness; it is simultaneously intellectual and intuitive. It places a premium on individuality, and yet a jazz group is a model of cooperation and coordination.

A jazz group is not just a collection of different instruments, as one might think of classical music, but a collection of different sensibilities that come together and are applied to the same material. It is the tension among those sensibilities that produces the character of a jazz performance. Obviously, if you have indistinct sensibilities, the performance will lack dynamic tension or character. Jazz, you might say, is *all* interpretation. It is all about point of view; in literary terms, it takes place in the first person, present tense.

∿∿∿

Jazz is primarily to be heard, to be experienced. This book is accompanied by a compact disc containing seven performances by some of jazz's greatest musicians. Each of these performances illustrates the points made in the text, and the text contains time markings to allow you to locate the specific moments being discussed on each track.

If you are new to jazz, you may want to listen to the CD before reading the text. No words can convey the exciting interplay among the instruments on King Oliver's "Weather Bird Rag"; the buoyancy of Jimmy Rushing's blues vocal, Count Basie's piano, and Lester Young's tenor saxophone on "Boogie Woogie"; the sub-

tlety of Duke Ellington's orchestration as it sets off Dizzy Gillespie's trumpet on "U.M.M.G."; Sonny Rollins's improvising ingenuity on "Moritat"; Stan Getz's amazing subtlety and grace on "I
Can't Get Started"; the intensity and hothouse complexity of the
rhythms and textures on Miles Davis's "Footprints"; and the flat-
out exhilaration on "The Eternal Triangle," where Dizzy Gillespie,
Sonny Rollins, and Sonny Stitt meet and square off in an unforgettable jam session.

After you've listened, the text can help you begin to understand
and recognize patterns in the music. One can enjoy watching a
basketball game (the grace, the coordination, the feints, the timing and communication among team members) without knowing
the principles of good basketball that guide play on the court, but
knowing something about them can help one appreciate not just
the kinetic action but also the strategy involved in the game.

So this book's six chapters provide a series of ways to look at
these performances, and at almost all jazz performances. Although technical questions are discussed, sometimes in considerable detail, the text is designed to be understood even by readers
who have no musical training at all.

Briefly, then, here is an overview of the book's structure. Chapter 1, "Foreground and Background," discusses the ways in which
individual instruments or voices in a jazz performance relate to
an overall group effect. Chapter 2 looks at the blues, both as a
form of music—simple and endlessly flexible—and as a body of
expressive techniques that have been basic to jazz since its beginnings. Chapter 3, "Forms," expands on "Blues" by looking at other
structures that jazz musicians use, especially the various forms
found in the American popular songs that have made up the main
jazz repertoire for most of its history.

Within any given form, how does a jazz musician decide what notes to play? Chapter 4, "Improvisation," shows how most jazz performances are based on an underlying harmonic skeleton, a sort of code that allows the musicians to make sense even while improvising spontaneously. Chapter 5, "Swing, Rhythm, Time, Space," looks at that most characteristic and elusive quality of jazz performance, the rhythmic lift usually called "swing," as well as at the way time changes quality during musical performance. And Chapter 6, "Telling a Story," looks at the qualities that give jazz musicians individual sounds and styles—at expression, the least codifiable and ultimately most precious element of them all.

Of course, no one book or disc can tell you everything you want or need to know about jazz. So you will find at the end of each chapter an extensive listing of recorded performances that further illustrate the points and questions raised in that chapter. In the interest of keeping these lists manageable, I have cut off the listings at about 1970, which has meant having to ignore many fine later examples. But this approach has, at least, the advantage of steering you to classic recordings in the idiom, the foundation of everything that came after. There are several guidebooks to recordings that deal with post-1970 work in exhaustive detail, most notably *The Penguin Guide to Jazz.*

This being said, it is important to remember that jazz still goes on and still changes, and there are no limits on what musicians' imaginations will come up with. Jazz music has always incorporated all kinds of music, and it has also encountered all kinds of influences over the course of its history. Jazz musicians play in all kinds of contexts today, with musicians from all kinds of traditions—bluegrass, rock, Latin, Arabic, classical, and much more.

What, finally, makes jazz jazz? There is no definitive answer to that. Some find the question itself an annoyance, an irrelevancy. It may be best to remember, as we try to understand any form, that the borders of such terms and categories are extremely porous. It may be a good thing to be suspicious of any stylistic term when it is used too loudly. Individual artists rarely love the stylistic categories applied to them. But as long as we use the word, we may as well ask ourselves what we mean by it—being aware, all the while, that any attempt at crystallizing a definition will likely be met with an avalanche of exceptions. And that, to a large degree, is how we know that the form is still living and breathing.

Tom Piazza

New Orleans, March 2005

Understanding

Miles Davis Quintet, 1964. From left: Wayne Shorter, tenor saxophone; Ron Carter, bass; Herbie Hancock, piano; Tony Williams, drums; Miles Davis, trumpet.
Photograph by Jan Persson, courtesy of CTSImages.

One

Foreground and Background

Although it is possible to play jazz music solo (especially on the piano, where one can accompany oneself), most jazz music is played by groups of musicians. Jazz is always, as the great pianist Bill Evans once remarked, "a social situation"; it involves a number of musicians speaking a shared language, but with highly individual sensibilities.

One of the first questions to ask in trying to understand any social situation is, How is it organized? That is, what are the implicit or explicit ground rules that guide the interactions among the members? If we look at the history of jazz, we see an astonishing variety of answers to this question. But underneath those answers run some common threads.

In jazz, or in most music of any type, there is usually some kind of relationship between a lead voice, or voices—whether instrumental or vocal—and an accompaniment, just as in representational painting there is some relationship between the objects that are the main focus of interest and all the elements that populate the space around those objects. Another way of putting this might be to say that there is a relationship between the voice of the individual and the voice(s) of the community in which the individual operates.

That relationship, or set of relationships, has taken many forms in jazz. It might exist between a clearly defined lead voice and clearly defined accompanists, such as that between Sonny Rollins's tenor saxophone lead and the accompaniment of the piano, bass, and drums on "Moritat" (track 4 on the accompanying CD); or it might be a somewhat more entwined, symbiotic relationship, like that between Stan Getz's tenor saxophone and Kenny Barron's piano on "I Can't Get Started" (track 5); or it might be a solo horn against a written-out ensemble accompaniment, as in the collaboration between Dizzy Gillespie's trumpet and the Duke Ellington Orchestra on "U.M.M.G." (track 3); or any number of other permutations.

Jazz is a music of highly individual sensibilities. A jazz ensemble consists not just of different instruments but of the different, contrasting musical personalities of its players. Much of the craft that jazz musicians acquire is there to help them develop an unmistakable voice. And a jazz group is organized to give those individual voices the greatest possible opportunity to express themselves while still being coordinated as an ensemble. The group effect depends on the tension among its individual sensibilities.

In fact, even though much jazz places heavy emphasis on the improvisations of a soloist, it is good to learn how to listen to all the instruments in an ensemble at once, to learn to hear the entire group as an interdependent organism. A soloist doesn't exist in a vacuum; the soloist will be responding to everything that is happening while he or she is improvising, just as the accompanists will be responding not only to the soloist but to one another, in an ongoing conversation. The pianist will respond to the drummer's rhythmic accents, the soloist will hear the chords the pianist plays and react harmonically, and so on. The best jazz will reward one's listening to it as if to a unified field of sound, with shifting foreground and background elements.

In jazz's New Orleans beginnings, this fact sits at the center of the music. In classic New Orleans jazz, such as that heard in King Oliver's recording of "Weather Bird Rag" (track 1), there is less made of the distinction between the solo voice and the background than there is in some other types of jazz. Jazz in its early days in New Orleans was the product of a tightly knit yet varied community, and in a sense the music reflects the kinds of situations in which it was used—street parades, dances, community celebrations. Each voice in the group contributes to an overall sound composed of individuals celebrating the same occasion, each in his or her own way. Each horn, rather than playing an individual solo in series, simultaneously plays a series of spontaneous variations on the same theme, organized in a very specific way.

In fact, contemporary ears may be so used to hearing a sharp distinction between foreground and background, between a solo voice and its accompaniment, that a performance such as "Weather Bird Rag" may come as something of a shock. In it, almost every instrumental voice, certainly every wind instrument, seems to be in the foreground at the same time.

King Oliver's Creole Jazz Band was one of the greatest ensembles in jazz history, and it represented the high-water mark of classic New Orleans–style jazz. With its "front line" of two cornets, trombone, and clarinet, and accompaniment by piano, banjo, and drummer Baby Dodds playing woodblocks, it generated an irresistible momentum as well as a profound equilibrium, one in which all the parts contributed to the totality of sound. Recorded in 1923, "Weather Bird Rag" captures the Oliver band at a period when they were influencing every young musician in Chicago, where they presided at the Lincoln Gardens. The leader, cornetist Joseph "King" Oliver, was one of the great instrumentalists to come out of New Orleans, and he surrounded himself with many of the best younger players, especially his protégé, the very young Louis Armstrong. Armstrong, in fact, plays cornet alongside Oliver on "Weather Bird Rag," which is Armstrong's composition as well.

Once our ears get used to the limited acoustic range, we can hear something like a musical miracle in progress. All the musicians are playing at once, each is playing something different, and yet the music doesn't sound chaotic. There is a unified effect consisting of very disparate elements. How is this possible?

The New Orleans musicians achieved this alchemy in part by adhering to a specific division of labor among the wind instruments. In the classic New Orleans ensemble, as exemplified by the Oliver band and other early ensembles such as the Original Dixieland Jazz Band and the New Orleans Rhythm Kings, those instruments are typically the trumpet (or cornet), the trombone, and the clarinet. Each is assigned a role in which it contributes a distinct element to the overall musical texture. Within these respective roles there is considerable room for spontaneous variation, or improvisation, but the difference in the nature of each contribution keeps the overall texture from becoming muddy or jumbled. Simply put, here is how they divide things up.

In a New Orleans band, the trumpet or cornet will typically play the main melody, or the lead. The trumpet fills this role for two basic reasons. Being made of brass, the trumpet is very loud—it can be heard over what everyone else is playing—and it is pitched more or less in the range of the human voice, which makes it ideal for, in a sense, "singing" the melody.

The trombone, also made of brass, is also loud, but it is pitched lower than the trumpet; it sits more naturally in a chestier, more guttural register. It is less flexible than the trumpet in terms of execution, due to the necessity of using the slide, a somewhat awkward way of achieving different pitches compared to the trumpet's valves, which are worked with three fingers and can be manipulated more fluidly. So, due to its somewhat cumbersome quality and its lower range, the trombone tends to play simpler phrases in a lower register. The trombone plays held notes as well as short, rhythmic phrases, and acts as a foil for the trumpet melody.

Finally, the clarinet is made of wood and generates its tones by means of a vibrating reed made of cane (as opposed to the brass instruments, in which the player's lips vibrate inside a small, cup-shaped mouthpiece), so it contributes a distinct tonal coloration against the two brass instruments. In addition, because of its construction, the clarinet can play fluid, multinote melodic lines with relative ease, and this is what it does most often in the New Orleans ensemble. As the trumpet plays its variations on the main melody and the trombone plays its shorter, simpler phrases, the clarinet spins a lacy filigree of notes that wind all over, under, and around what the other instruments play; its sinuous lines curl, like cigarette smoke, into every available nook and cranny of the music.

As long as these three instruments stay more or less in their respective roles, they are free to contribute a fair amount of individual variation—to improvise—and they can do so without, in a sense, stepping on one another's lines. They are like actors adlibbing a scene: They know their respective parts so well that they can make spontaneous variations while remaining in character and moving the scene forward.

Of course, in practice, groups rarely adhere to this division of labor all the way through a performance. For the sake of variety, there are times when each instrument may come to the foreground in different ways, as you will hear in "Weather Bird Rag." The two cornets, for example, can plainly be heard playing different things—simultaneous variations on the song's melody. There are times in other Oliver performances when, for variety, the clarinet or the trombone might assume the lead for a while. But the basic arrangement remains the norm. The effect is something like watching a New Orleans parade roll down a street, followed by a long "second line" of dancers, each improvising his or her own steps to the music of the brass band.

And yet the individual parts are not totally subsumed in an ensemble effect. Notice how, at various points, the entire ensemble stops abruptly for several beats while an individual instrument plays a brief statement, and then resumes. This device is called a "break." In "Weather Bird Rag," each instrument except the piano takes a brief break—trombone, clarinet, banjo, even the ticktocky woodblocks played by Baby Dodds. Notice that the two cornets take their breaks (at the 2:09 mark as well as at the very end of the tune) together. Breaks are usually thought of as a way for an instrumentalist to demonstrate quick reflexes, imagination on the spur of the moment, but they can also be planned in advance, as

Oliver and Armstrong plainly did here—they play the same melodic figure in harmony. These kinds of breaks, by the way, caused a sensation during the band's reign in Chicago. Still, in general, these performances are about the ensemble rather than about individual solo prowess.

Some musicians in other eras and styles of jazz have been fascinated with the possibilities for group improvisation on the New Orleans model, although not as many as one might think. One of the primary examples was the bassist and composer Charles Mingus, who loved to set his horn players against one another so that they would improvise simultaneously. See "Further Listening" at the end of this chapter for other examples.

~~~

For most of jazz's history, though, there has been a sharper and more deliberate distinction drawn between foreground and background elements. To a large extent, this was the result of the stunning example laid down by the flowering of Louis Armstrong's improvising genius in his recordings and performances of the mid-1920s. Inspired by Armstrong's example on his recordings with the big band of Fletcher Henderson as well as his slightly later Hot Five and Hot Seven recordings, musicians became fascinated with the possibilities of playing extended solos. Other musicians besides Armstrong were developing strong individual solo improvising sensibilities in the early 1920s as well, to be sure— among them the clarinetist and soprano saxophonist Sidney Bechet and the cornetist Bix Beiderbecke—but it was Armstrong's influence above all that made it *necessary* for young musicians to develop the ability to play solos.

Armstrong in effect handed down a kind of improvisational

grammar, a logic of fitting certain kinds of phrases to certain kinds of harmonic formations that proved to be so useful that countless musicians—on all instruments, not only the trumpet—constructed distinct and identifiable styles on the basis of that grammar. The latter half of the 1920s saw an explosion of individual improvisational voices based on that language. Trumpeters Joe Smith, Rex Stewart, Muggsy Spanier, Cootie Williams, Jabbo Smith, Wingy Manone, Henry "Red" Allen, Charlie Teagarden, Max Kaminsky, and slightly later, players such as Bunny Berigan, Harry James, and Jonah Jones wove their own styles out of Armstrong's language, much as a later generation would do with the grammar that alto saxophonist Charlie Parker perfected in the 1940s.

During that same period of the 1920s, what might seem like exactly the opposite impulse also came to the fore: a fascination with the possibilities of orchestrating jazz for larger ensembles, in which musicians would play written-out parts that would have the rhythmic impetus of jazz. This approach produced a broad spectrum of work, from Jelly Roll Morton's Red Hot Peppers recordings, in which pianist-composer Morton wrote out parts for a typical New Orleans small-band configuration, to Fletcher Henderson and his arrangers, who took the large dance band of the day, with its division into trumpet, trombone, and woodwind "sections," and turned it to jazz purposes, and to Paul Whiteman's arrangers, especially Bill Challis, who used jazz's syncopations sparingly for a mammoth large orchestra, laced with Impressionist harmony and leaving space for brief solos by jazz musicians.

Still, for most jazz fans, it is the exciting interplay of a soloist spinning spontaneous variations on a form against the commentary and support of a rhythm section that forms the heart of jazz.

What jazz musicians call the rhythm section is most commonly the little constellation of piano, bass, and drums. "Rhythm section" is a slightly misleading term for this grouping, since the piano and bass function not just to set the tempo and provide rhythmic accents but also to outline the harmonic background of the song. The drums, while playing a more strictly rhythmic role, may also add coloristic and even melodic elements at times (as Tony Williams does throughout Miles Davis's "Footprints," track 6). And any of the rhythm-section instruments can take over the lead or solo role for a spell. So the "accompaniment" plays a more active and integrated role in the music than it may initially seem to.

That relationship, between the "foreground" of the soloist and the "background" of the rhythm section, has shifted over the course of jazz and among its practitioners. In some styles and with some ensembles, the relationship is truly that of soloist with support; the rhythm section, for the most part, is there to abet the improvisations of the soloist, to surround a very clear foreground element with commentary that will enhance the main line of the soloist's thought, and even give the soloist fodder to further his or her improvisations. This is generally the case in "Boogie Woogie," "Moritat," and "The Eternal Triangle."

"Boogie Woogie" (track 2), recorded in 1936 by a small contingent from the Count Basie Orchestra, is a perfect illustration of this relationship. The main theme is simple enough: Carl Smith's trumpet plays a peppery little two-note "call," and Lester Young's tenor sax provides an ascending "response." These phrases are what jazz musicians call "riffs"—short, repeated phrases whose main function is to create forward rhythmic momentum. Often, riffs are also used behind soloists, to build excitement or to vary the texture, as they do at points during "Boogie Woogie."

You can hear clearly, once Jimmy Rushing begins his buoyant vocal, the way the lead voice and the background interact. The bass and drums are there to set the rhythm and keep it going; the bass additionally outlines the harmonic background. On top of them, Count Basie's piano plays jabbing, exhortatory chords, especially after the ends of Rushing's phrases, a kind of response to the call of the vocal line. This pattern continues after the instrumental soloists begin their improvisations. Once Lester Young's solo starts, not only Basie's piano but also Jo Jones's drums contribute accents and commentary, in the manner of a church congregation punctuating a sermon with amens. The texture thickens even more when trumpeter Smith begins his solo (played with a mute in the horn). Here Young adds saxophone riffs behind the solo.

This kind of jazz group is really a microcosm of the approach taken by some of the more jazz-inflected big bands of that period, usually known as the swing era. There was a balance achieved during the 1930s between the grace and imagination of the soloists and the sense of group texture and coherence that was the heart of the swing era. Such bands usually played for dancing as well as for listening. The forward-moving, dance-oriented rhythm is a constant factor underneath the successive statements by the solo voices. The soloists play with, and around, the rhythm, but the rhythm is a given, and that forward movement is never really questioned, as it would be in some later approaches to jazz. The soloist here is, in a sense, an expression of the group, the collaborative project—a large part of which was the discovery of how to dominate forward-moving time itself, to keep equilibrium and be inventive against a metrical background.

On tenor saxophonist Sonny Rollins's 1956 reworking of Kurt

Weill's "Moritat" (track 4), better known as "Mack the Knife," the same relationship exists between the saxophone and the rhythm section as in "Boogie Woogie"—the saxophone spins a solo and the rhythm section keeps time underneath, feeding the soloist harmonic and rhythmic ideas as they go.

The most immediately noticeable difference is a quantitative one—Rollins's solo goes on much longer than Lester Young's. This is due in part to developments in recording technology; the typical 10-inch, 78-rpm disc of the 1920s through the 1940s, on which "Weather Bird Rag" and "Boogie Woogie" were recorded, could fit only about three minutes on a side. The introduction, in the early 1950s, of long-playing record technology made it possible to capture more extended performances—as much as half an hour on a side—than were possible on the earlier discs.

But the length of "Moritat" also reflects a shift that occurred in the aesthetics of jazz music. The focus of serious jazz performance by this time was often almost entirely on a soloist's ability to create an extended improvisation, as opposed to the soloist being another part of a group that was furnishing music basically for dancing.

In private, musicians have always liked to play extended improvised solos. In informal jam sessions, they improvise for their mutual amusement, work out ideas, and learn from one another. But in the 1920s and 1930s, the public face of the music in performance was still rooted in the communal experience of dancing. Jazz music still functioned most often as one part of a larger social situation, a fabric of which the music was just one element.

But World War II brought tremendous social upheavals. Big bands became much harder to sustain economically. People from different regions of the United States and different parts of the culture were thrown together in the armed services and in the rapidly swelling cities in ways they never had been before. Society was becoming more complex, and almost in an echo of that complexity, jazz's spotlight began to shift slightly away from the communal experience of dancers and ensembles to the individual soloist who would match himself or herself against increasingly complex background settings. By just so much, an element of theater entered the mix, or moved closer to the center of the mix. Jazz was turning into a theater of creativity and chance taking, like watching a high-wire act or a sporting event that involved more than just physical eloquence. This had always been part of the show in jazz, even from the beginning, but it was to become almost the whole show—for a while, at least.

In "Moritat," the focus is almost entirely on the astonishing inventiveness and ingenuity of tenor saxophonist Sonny Rollins, who is a continual font of ideas as he spins out his improvisations on top of the subtle and responsive rhythm section. As he plays, the rhythm section responds to what he plays, and he is challenged, in turn, to make use of the things he hears them play. In good jazz, the playing situation is rarely as simple as a pure foreground and a pure background. For one example, after Rollins's melody statement, at around 0:45, listen to drummer Max Roach keeping time first on the hi-hat and then on the ride cymbal, like a car shifting gears, as Rollins begins his improvisation, and notice how it affects the feel of the music.

Notice also how pianist Tommy Flanagan plays sharp, rhythmically inflected chords, like little "amen"s or "uh-huh"s, like the responses of a church congregation to the words of a preacher, behind Rollins's saxophone solo, as Count Basie did behind Lester

Young twenty years earlier. These chords serve both a harmonic and a rhythmic purpose; they outline the harmony as it shifts, and they goad Rollins's imagination, answering his phrases as well as suggesting new ideas to him. Flanagan is very clearly filling a supporting role during the saxophone solo, but when Rollins is finished, Flanagan steps to center stage and takes his own solo.

After Flanagan's solo, Rollins comes back in for a kind of conversation with drummer Max Roach, a dialogue consisting of alternating improvised four-bar phrases. Musicians usually refer to this as "trading fours." It is another face of the emphasis on inventiveness and spontaneous imagination; the idea is to have a match of wits between two (or more) instrumentalists in which they trade ideas and, often, try to outdo each other in inventiveness and dexterity. Musicians will also commonly do this with alternating eight-bar phrases ("trading eights"), two-bar phrases, and so on. After the exchanges, Roach goes into a drum solo, and when he is finished, bassist Doug Watkins takes his own solo. Notice that no matter who is playing a solo, everyone else either recedes into a supporting role or drops out entirely. The focus, in other words, is squarely on whoever is soloing at the moment.

For a fascinating contrast, listen to Stan Getz's recording of "I Can't Get Started" (track 5)—also a tenor saxophonist with a rhythm section playing a standard. Beyond the fact that in Getz's hands, the tenor saxophone sounds like a completely different instrument than it does in Rollins's, notice how Getz's extremely lyrical improvisation seems to exist as an ongoing, full-fledged dialogue with the piano of Kenny Barron, whose commentary is almost an equal part of the foreground with the saxophone soloist. Getz also leaves more "space" in his solo—openings where he doesn't play for a beat or two or three—giving room for Barron to comment more extensively. This is possible partly because of the much slower tempo.

Throughout, listen closely to the way in which Getz responds to what Barron plays, and vice versa. There are far too many instances of perfect sympathy and cooperation to begin singling them out; listen, and you will hear. One passage among many begins at around 5:36, where Getz ends a phrase with a little two-note descending figure that he repeats, in a different register and altered harmonically; Barron hears him and responds by playing a similar two-note descending phrase in chords; Getz hears that and responds in turn, and they spin a lovely duet out of that motif until the end of Getz's solo.

This setup obviously places a high premium on an active dialogue between the saxophone and the piano. This dialogue is so striking and beautiful here that one might miss the very subtle ways in which drummer Victor Lewis varies his accompaniment, played with brushes rather than sticks, and also the ways in which bassist Rufus Reid maintains the pulse while playing around it. This quartet, while keeping a more or less traditional relationship between the soloist and the background, brings the two elements closer together and integrates them more than in "Moritat." The overall sound and collaborative nature of the interplay is the central point, rather than just a string of soloists in succession. Notice also, as if to underscore this point, that the performance ends on the piano, which drifts off into never-never land without the saxophone ever coming back.

～～～

We are in a different neighborhood with the Miles Davis Quintet's classic 1966 recording of "Footprints" (track 6). During the 1960s many groups ratcheted up the relationship between the background and the foreground even further. Not just piano but bass and drums often became part of the music's foreground. In the groups of John Coltrane, Ornette Coleman, Charles Mingus, and Miles Davis, probably the four most important bandleaders of that period, the possibilities of group interplay were hashed out and experimented with and shifted around in many different and provocative ways. Often the drums became very prominent; this was especially true in the groups of Coltrane and Davis, whose drummers—Elvin Jones and Tony Williams, respectively—were innovators and great creative forces in their own right.

This is what we hear on "Footprints." Each part of the group is a crucial element of the shifting compositional texture of the performance. The recording begins with a little repeated figure from bassist Ron Carter, which continues throughout and is the rhythmic trunk around which everything else entwines. After the chantlike theme, composed by the group's saxophonist, Wayne Shorter, Davis plays a very aggressive trumpet solo full of rhythmic thrusts and parries against the stark chords of Herbie Hancock's piano and, especially, the chittering, shifting drum commentary from Tony Williams.

Hancock's piano chords function as more than just commentary on a soloist's line; he is setting up his own patterns as a foreground element, against and through which Davis's trumpet moves. Williams's drums, too, are their own foreground structure, certainly not just a timekeeping function behind a soloist's line of thought. In fact, throughout the track, Williams keeps shifting the rhythmic feel of the music; sometimes he seems to be playing a fast tempo, sometimes a slow, walking tempo, other times almost a kind of Latin beat. The bass functions as a root, playing that repeated phrase against a basic pulse, but against that pulse many different rhythms can be played.

In the Davis band of that time, everyone in the group was encouraged to think about these simultaneous rhythmic possibilities, and the performance became a kaleidoscopically shifting theater of rhythmic and harmonic alternatives, with all the members contributing to a constantly mutating shared reality. The point, for this chapter, is that the implicitly hierarchical relationship between foreground soloist and background accompaniment was less meaningful in this context; the point of the music was to have everyone in the band taking an active role not only in perpetuating the momentum of the rhythmic and harmonic understructure while the soloist played, but in steering the overall shape of the performance.

All these elements, it should be noted, are a matter of degree. Good soloists in jazz always respond to what the rhythm section plays, as we have seen, and the rhythm section always responds to the soloist's unfolding improvisation. But in a recording such as "Footprints," the entire shape and direction of the music changes and shifts as the members of the group tug and pull and block and extend, like a cloud of birds over a field getting larger, hovering, suddenly swooping in a different direction, stretching out and then bunching up in a cloud. It is a true collaborative composition, involving the full creative energies of everyone in the ensemble.

Duke Ellington's 1959 recording of the Billy Strayhorn composition "U.M.M.G." (track 3) presents yet another set of coordinates. Here, in addition to soloist with rhythm section, we have the additional factor of other horns, arranged in sections and playing from a written score. The foreground and background are determined not so much by convention or group improvisation as by the mind of the composer and arranger—in this case, Ellington's creative partner Billy Strayhorn. The track presents a carefully orchestrated, progressive relationship not only between the main solo voice—the trumpet of Dizzy Gillespie, who was sitting in as guest soloist with the band—and the rhythm section, but between the soloist and the trumpet, trombone, and saxophone sections of the Ellington orchestra.

After a brief piano introduction, the track gets rolling with Gillespie playing a kind of abstract of the theme, alone, accompanied only by bass and drums. At around 1:28, if you listen closely, you will hear a slight shift in what the bass and drums play, setting the stage for the entry of a new element, the band itself. The saxophones enter playing the theme, with commentary from a muted brass choir; in the middle of their reading of the theme, which gets louder as it goes along, clarinetist Jimmy Hamilton plays a solo with commentary from the saxophone section behind him.

As the performance goes on, Gillespie comes back, without the mute now, drummer Sam Woodyard shifting to a different cymbal and the saxophones playing commentary behind him. Notice how the phrases the saxophones play behind Gillespie's solos function very similarly to the piano accompaniments on "Boogie Woogie" and "Moritat"—a series of "amen"s and "uh-huh"s meant to goad the soloist.

This section then gives way to another, and then another; the trombone section alternating with Harry Carney's baritone saxophone and Gillespie's trumpet, the entire performance getting louder. Back and forth it goes; the rhythm section is certainly in a very traditional "background" role, but the orchestrated voices of the saxophone, trombone, and trumpet sections work both as background to soloists and as foreground elements in their own right. All of these shifts were carefully orchestrated, planned out in advance, by Ellington and Strayhorn.

Here the voice of the "community," or ensemble, has a different meaning than it had in the small-group performances we have looked at. At times the band's various sections function as accompaniment for the solo voice, at times they are in a call-and-response relationship with it, and at times they themselves constitute the lead. The foreground and background are constantly shifting, but under the direction of one organizing intelligence: that of the composer and arranger. The "background" provides the meaning of the performance, the context against which the solo voice functions. In this particular performance, there is a heavy emphasis on Gillespie's improvising solo voice, but the context of the background is the real point of the performance; it constructs an arc of meaning that has been literally orchestrated by a composer.

When jazz is played by large ensembles, it is almost inevitable that an orchestrator will be necessary to provide written parts. The flexibility and independence of a small group with only a couple of horns and a rhythm section is not possible when a band has three or more saxophones, a couple of trombones, and several trumpets. Some big bands, most famously Count Basie's, managed to work out schemes by which the sections could confer quietly while a performance was in progress and set riffs behind soloists, or otherwise develop a rudimental sectional interplay without written parts. But most large bands need the services of an orchestrator. Jazz has had many important composers and arrangers, including Duke Ellington, Billy Strayhorn, Gil Evans, Gerry Mulligan, Benny Carter, George Russell, and Charles Mingus. A number of their recordings will be listed and briefly discussed in "Further Listening" at the end of this chapter.

~~~

With Dizzy Gillespie's recording of "The Eternal Triangle" (track 7), we are back with the assumptions of "Moritat," but in the foreground is another dramatic element, that of competition between two equal voices. Sonny Rollins reappears here, matched up with fellow tenor saxophonist Sonny Stitt, for a "tenor battle," in this case one of the greatest ever recorded. This performance is, in fact, very close to the spirit of the jam session, the informal gatherings where musicians would play off of one another, sometimes competitively, sometimes collaboratively, and often both.

Here the focus is unequivocally on the battle of wits between two closely matched soloists. The rhythm section is there to goad them on, to provide a steady and inspiring background, to keep the rhythm and harmony in place, shifting just enough to make things interesting but never competing for foreground attention with the soloists. In this case, the foreground gains its character in large measure from the two tenors in close proximity; in fact, nearly everything in the first nine minutes of this performance is designed to set them off, one against the other, in a test of equilibrium, coordination, imagination, and wit. This is a "community" in which spontaneous intelligence and wit and prowess are central values and are tested constantly. The soloist's background or context is not only the rhythm section but also the imaginative world of the other soloists.

But in this kind of contest, the proceedings are not enhanced by a clear victory. The hope is that each voice will prod the other to greater feats of concentration and dexterity and wit, in which everyone will come out the winner. Notice how, during solos, the horns that aren't soloing will periodically set up a riff behind the solo voice to generate more excitement and momentum (during Rollins's solo this happens at 1:32; during Stitt's at 4:10; during Gillespie's trumpet solo at 10:11), underscoring the communal nature of the endeavor.

Another feature of this performance is the section of rapid-fire exchanges between Rollins and Stitt. After long solos from each of them (Rollins first, from the end of the opening ensemble until about 2:55, when Stitt enters for his solo, which lasts until 6:21), they begin a long section of alternating statements of 4 bars apiece, going back and forth and each building on the phrases the other played, in a high-voltage display of imagination and quick reflexes. At 7:37 they shift to 8-bar exchanges, giving each player slightly greater room to stretch out in their statements. The foreground here is all about this match of wits.

At 8:54 Dizzy Gillespie comes in for his trumpet solo. If you listen closely, you will notice that for the first 16 bars of Gillespie's solo, the bass plays the same note over and over underneath the trumpet, creating a mounting tension, which releases as they go into the tune's middle section, or "bridge" (see chapter 3 for a fuller explanation of this term). After Gillespie's solo, pianist Ray Bryant has a brief solo before Gillespie comes back in for a series of exchanges with drummer Charlie Persip.

"The Eternal Triangle" brings us about as close as we can get to an apotheosis of the individual improvising soloist as hero, a theater of spontaneous intelligence, alertness, organizing ability, and coordination that is not that far in some ways from the values of an athletic event. The listener is amazed, entertained, and refreshed by witnessing prodigies of concentration and wit, deftness and stamina; one is reminded that such coordination and grace is possible not just in theory but in practice, in the real world of passing time and mortality.

We have seen seven different ways of working out the relations between the individual intelligence and the need for group coherence. You can believe that there are many more. But the working out of that balance, the project of that kind of dialogue and interrelationship between an individual and a community of other voices, is one of the most central and important things about jazz music. "Further Listening" will suggest some other points of departure.

Further Listening:
Foreground and Background

The following recordings have been singled out because they show something especially interesting or representative about the possibilities for group interaction in jazz. This is by no means intended to be an exhaustive list of important jazz-ensemble recordings—although it may seem like one!—but merely an initial set of suggestions of significant recordings for further listening. Because of the extent and breadth of the subject in this chapter, this will be the longest such list in the book. Of all the elements of jazz, the question of the way in which ensembles have been organized bears the most heavily on the question of how the music has developed over its history.

~~~

To really understand the New Orleans style, the 1923–24 King Oliver Creole Jazz Band recordings are the place to start. The Creole Jazz Band's combination of propulsion and equilibrium was never matched; the various instruments filled their roles perfectly. These recordings, made originally for the small labels Gennett and OKeh, are available today on compact disc in many forms. "Just Gone," "Canal Street Blues," "Dippermouth Blues," "Chimes Blues," "Weather Bird Rag," "I Ain't Gonna Tell Nobody," and all the rest represent the most perfect expression of the classic New Orleans style.

The 1917 recordings by the Original Dixieland Jazz Band (RCA/BMG) are raucous and full of life and fun and are worth hearing. This is what the world outside New Orleans first heard when it heard "jazz," and many of the songs they introduced, including "Tiger Rag," "Original Dixieland One-Step," and "Sensation Rag," became staples of the jazz repertoire for years after. The New Orleans Rhythm Kings' early-1920s recordings (originally recorded for Gennett and now available on various imported labels) are also seminal recordings in this style, as are the recordings of Sam Morgan's Jazz Band and Oscar "Papa" Celestin's Tuxedo Jazz Band, originally recorded for Columbia and currently available together on the Canadian Jazz Oracle label.

Louis Armstrong's Hot Five and Hot Seven recordings, from between 1926 and 1928 (Columbia/Legacy), show in microcosm the development and integration of a solo sensibility into what was still essentially a New Orleans context. The earliest Hot Fives— "My Heart," "Heebie Jeebies," "Muskrat Ramble"—sound much like stripped-down Creole Jazz Band performances. But as the sessions progressed, Armstrong and the other soloists get more and more room, especially Louis, whose virtuosity and imagination and personality increasingly move to the center of the frame, become the *point* of what's going on. Landmark recordings such as "Cornet Chop Suey," "Struttin' with Some Barbecue," "Potato Head Blues," "Weary Blues," "Wild Man Blues" (these last three not, formally speaking, blues, despite their titles; see chapter 2 for a discussion of the blues), and "Willie the Weeper" all contain fabulous, imaginative improvised solos by Armstrong, along with flat-out New Orleans ensembles, including the likes of trombonist Kid Ory and clarinetist Johnny Dodds.

For a fascinating comparison with the King Oliver recording of

"Weather Bird Rag," listen to Armstrong's 1928 recording of "Weather Bird" (Columbia/Legacy), played as a duet with piano innovator Earl Hines. Here there are only two instruments, trumpet and piano, yet there is that same quality of multiple simultaneous lines of musical thought constantly playing off against each other. Armstrong plays variations on the trumpet lead as Hines's piano provides an allusive, almost Cubist, summoning of all the other possible parts of the music—rhythm, clarinet filigree, bold trombone figures—dancing around Armstrong's ringing horn.

The third crucial figure in New Orleans jazz was the composer, pianist, and raconteur Jelly Roll Morton. In 1926 Morton began a series of recordings with a shifting repertory company of musicians, most of whom were, initially, from New Orleans. Over the next four years or so, Jelly Roll Morton and his Red Hot Peppers, as he called his band, made some of the most remarkable recordings of New Orleans jazz extant (RCA/BMG). In most of the best of these, Morton wrote out every note for his musicians to play, producing an orchestrated, notated version of New Orleans polyphony in which each interlude, break, dynamic shift, and even solo was carefully planned to create an overall effect. The earliest recordings were done by bands with a typical New Orleans configuration of trumpet, trombone, clarinet, piano, banjo, bass, and drums. Performances of songs such as "Black Bottom Stomp," "The Chant," "Sidewalk Blues," "Kansas City Stomps," and "Mr. Jelly Lord" are brilliantly and precisely crafted miniatures that contain an extraordinary expressive range within the confines of the three-minute 78-rpm discs of the time.

Sidney Bechet, the New Orleans clarinetist and soprano saxophonist, made many recordings of classic New Orleans–style jazz during his recording career, which spanned nearly four decades.

Two very special sets that might be mentioned are the early-1920s recordings under the leadership of pianist Clarence Williams, on which Bechet is paired with Louis Armstrong—the titles include "Coal Cart Blues," "Santa Claus Blues," and, especially, two incendiary versions of "Cake Walking Babies from Home," which are like watching a fencing match on a high wire. These recordings may be found on a number of import labels and are worth searching out. The same has to be said for a hard-to-find but precious 1940 meeting between Bechet and cornetist Muggsy Spanier, recorded for the small Hot Jazz Club of America label and available only on small imported labels. But Bechet and Spanier, backed only by guitar and bass, have one of the best and most intimate New Orleans–style conversations ever recorded, both on New Orleans standards like "That's a Plenty" and on pop tunes like "Sweet Sue (Just You)."

∿∿∿

Musicians in other eras of jazz often tipped their hat to the New Orleans approach to group improvisation. One of those who kept returning to the concept was bassist and composer Charles Mingus. On "Folk Forms No. 1" (Candid), recorded in 1960, he leads a stripped-down ensemble consisting of Eric Dolphy's alto saxophone, Ted Curson's trumpet, and Dannie Richmond's drums through a wild 13-minute group improvisation that at times sounds very much like a New Orleans group jamming, and it is one of the best examples of this approach applied successfully in another stylistic neighborhood. Also, his classic album *Blues and Roots* (Atlantic) contains several tracks that employ a kind of New Orleans counterpoint.

In the 1930s, the swing era, musicians often made gestures back in the direction of the New Orleans jazz on which they had grown up. There are too many examples to list, but not to be missed are the marvelous performances of "Way Down Yonder in New Orleans" and "Them There Eyes" by the Kansas City Six (Commodore), a small group from the late-1930s Count Basie band including trumpeter Buck Clayton and saxophone innovator Lester Young in one of his rare recordings playing clarinet. "Swing Is Here" and "I Hope Gabriel Likes My Music" by Gene Krupa's Swing Band (RCA/BMG) have white-hot New Orleans–style ensemble sections by a 1936 band including Roy Eldridge on trumpet, Benny Goodman on clarinet, and the undersung Chu Berry on tenor saxophone, functioning, in a sense, as a second clarinet. Lastly, "Bouncing with Bean" (RCA/BMG), recorded by a small band led by tenor saxophone giant Coleman Hawkins in 1940, contains some very exciting collective improvisation.

Charlie Parker, the alto saxophone genius who helped contribute a new grammar to jazz in the 1940s, often seemed in his improvisations to be thinking in several melodic lines simultaneously; he would play a phrase and then play an answering phrase, as if in dialogue with himself. He also composed two tunes that consisted of contrapuntal lines for saxophone and trumpet—"Ah-Leu-Cha" and "Chasin' the Bird"—which he recorded with Miles Davis on trumpet (Savoy). Davis continued to play "Ah-Leu-Cha" with his own quintet after he became a leader in his own right; he recorded several versions with John Coltrane's tenor handling the saxophone part (Columbia/Legacy).

Many of the so-called avant-garde jazz players of the 1960s were fascinated with group improvisation as well. Probably the most successful sustained example of collective improvisation in this stylistic arena is the album *Free Jazz*, led by alto saxophonist Ornette Coleman (Atlantic). This 1960 recording matches up

Coleman's alto and the bass clarinet of Eric Dolphy, trumpeters Freddie Hubbard and Don Cherry, and a double rhythm section, with two basses (Scott La Faro and Charlie Haden) and two drummers (Ed Blackwell and Billy Higgins) in an extended and ingeniously organized group improvisation. This music is very challenging to listen to, in large measure because there is so much going on, pulling in so many directions, all at the same time. But the music here is as rewarding as it is challenging, and it must be heard by anyone with a serious interest in jazz.

~~~

Around the same time that Armstrong was developing his solo conception on the Hot Five recordings, and Morton was raising the New Orleans ensemble style to its most polished and sophisticated level, others were refining their ideas about how to orchestrate jazz music for the larger bands that had become popular for dancing in the 1920s. The pianist and arranger Fletcher Henderson had the first great jazz big band, on recordings at least, beginning in 1923. Henderson had the benefit, beyond his own skills, of the talents of arrangers such as his brother Horace Henderson and saxophonist Don Redman, an enormously influential musician of that time. The Henderson band developed to its best jazz expression the technique of having instruments play in sections—three trumpets, two trombones, and three or four saxophones, initially, which would play contrasting parts set off against one another to compelling and danceable effect. The written arrangements were riddled with openings for soloists to make improvised statements, and Henderson's band was an incubator of talent with no equal at that time. It was where Armstrong went when he first left Oliver's band, and other star soloists nurtured by Henderson over the two decades of his greatest activity included tenor saxophonists Coleman Hawkins, Ben Webster, and Chu Berry; trumpeters Roy Eldridge, Bobby Stark, Joe Smith, and Rex Stewart; and trombonists Jimmy Harrison and Benny Morton.

The three-disc set *A Study in Frustration* (Columbia/Legacy) contains the most complete picture of Henderson's career available. From early tracks featuring Armstrong as soloist, the set takes listeners through the complicated, technically demanding late-1920s arrangements, beginning with the classic "The Stampede," which contains the first great recorded solo by Coleman Hawkins. Later pieces such as Henderson's arrangement of Jelly Roll Morton's "King Porter Stomp" and Don Redman's reworking of the Oliver-Armstrong "Dippermouth Blues" (retitled "Sugarfoot Stomp") formed the basis of the great wave of popular big bands in the 1930s—in particular that of Benny Goodman, for whom Henderson provided quite a few arrangements.

While Henderson was blazing his trail, the bandleader Paul Whiteman was gaining a large audience with a more elaborately orchestrated form of jazz-laced popular music, often incorporating a string section and other nods in the direction of European salon and classical music. Although the jazz quotient was usually considerably lower in his music than it was in, say, Henderson's, in his most interesting late-1920s recordings (RCA/BMG), Whiteman and his arranger Bill Challis managed to open space for jazz soloists such as saxophonist Frank Trumbauer, trombonist Jack Teagarden, and the legendary cornetist Bix Beiderbecke. Beiderbecke and Trumbauer also made quite a few recordings on their own (Columbia/Legacy) that made use of highly arranged touches and represent an attempt to do something similar to what Morton was doing, albeit with a different stylistic spin. The music is more urban than Morton's, slicker, and with more nods in the direction of the music of Ravel and other contemporary European composers.

Duke Ellington was the greatest experimenter of all with the relation between foreground and background, solo voice and ensemble voice. In his extremely varied orchestrations one finds everything from loosely structured jammed tunes consisting mainly of strings of solos to extended works for full orchestra. But most of his oeuvre is occupied by compositions in which solo voice and exquisitely orchestrated ensembles exist in an ever-evolving conversation. Ellington, along with his close creative partner Billy Strayhorn, was often at his best when conceiving extraordinary settings for the many distinctive instrumentalists who populated his band. Again, there are far too many examples to list, but some not to be missed are "Concerto for Cootie" (RCA/BMG), a dialogue between trumpeter Cootie Williams and the full band that later became known as "Do Nothing Till You Hear from Me"; "Boy Meets Horn" (Columbia/Legacy), a feature for cornetist Rex Stewart; "All Too Soon" and "Cottontail" (RCA/BMG), both of which are features for tenor saxophonist Ben Webster; and the full score for the film *Anatomy of a Murder* (Columbia/Legacy), which sets off alto saxophonist Johnny Hodges, violinist Ray Nance, tenor saxophonist Paul Gonsalves, and other voices, including Ellington's own piano, against an ingeniously orchestrated tableau. Around 1940, Ellington began to feature his new bassist Jimmy Blanton as a full-fledged soloist on recordings such as "Jack the Bear," which brought that rhythm-section instrument to the foreground in an extremely influential way. But nearly everything Ellington did was a variation on a career-long meditation on the relation between the individual voice and the collective project.

Benny Goodman's orchestra was one of the most precise and,

at its best, exciting ensembles of the time, super-coordinated, well oiled, and fiery. The tracks on *The Birth of Swing* (*1935–1936*) (RCA/BMG) show his band at its most disciplined and are a kind of textbook of swing-era big-band jazz playing. The relations among the band's sections are crisp and defined. When they performed live, the band could raise the roof, as it does in broadcast performances included in *On the Air* (*1937–1938*) (Columbia/Legacy), in which soloists Harry James, Gene Krupa, and Goodman himself light a fire inspired by the band's exhilarating playing. Also not to be missed is Goodman's famous *Carnegie Hall Jazz Concert* (Columbia/Legacy), a landmark of big-band jazz. Count Basie's orchestra was perhaps the most swinging of the swing era, and the sides it recorded in the late 1930s and early 1940s, like "One O'Clock Jump," "Jumpin' at the Woodside," "Roseland Shuffle" (Decca/GRP), "Tickle Toe," and "Taxi War Dance" (Columbia/Legacy), show a strong emphasis on soloists such as Lester Young, trumpeters Buck Clayton and Harry Edison, and Basie's own laconic, epigrammatic piano. The spare, almost minimalist arrangements are designed for maximum dance propulsion without too much intricate orchestration.

The many small-group recordings of the 1930s show the spread of Louis Armstrong's solo conception, and the fascination with a soloist's ability to make compelling rhythmic variations over the rhythm section's propulsive background. Most of the soloists played with big bands and enjoyed having the expanded spotlight that a small-group setting afforded. Perhaps the most famous of these recordings are those by Benny Goodman's trio and quartet, featuring drummer Gene Krupa, pianist Teddy Wilson, and vibraphonist Lionel Hampton (RCA/BMG). Sometimes referred to as "chamber jazz," these great recordings, mostly of standard pop tunes such as "Stardust," "Moonglow," "Ida, Sweet as Apple Cider," and "Runnin' Wild," range from intimate, reflective, and conversational ballads to amazing virtuoso showpieces. Wilson's piano style was widely influential, and Hampton was the pioneer player of the vibraphone; together with the aggressive drumming of Krupa and Goodman's polished clarinet, these recordings exuded both poise and excitement.

Hampton and Wilson also made their own respective series of influential small-band recordings in the 1930s. Those led by Hampton (RCA/BMG) contained shifting personnel featuring many of the greatest musicians of the time, including saxophonists Coleman Hawkins, Chu Berry, Johnny Hodges, and Ben Webster; guitarist Charlie Christian; and trumpeters Dizzy Gillespie, Cootie Williams, and Henry "Red" Allen. Wilson's small-band recordings of the same period (Columbia/Legacy) featured many of the same players, often accompanying the great singer Billie Holiday. The Kansas City Six also made some classic recordings (Commodore). This group, joined by guitarist Charlie Christian, also performed at the famous late-1930s Spirituals to Swing concerts at Carnegie Hall, organized by impresario John Hammond; it was recorded and can be heard in a box set that includes performances from the same evenings by blues singers, a gospel quartet, boogie-woogie pianists, and more (Vanguard). Christian may also be heard on a series of recordings by the Benny Goodman Sextet (Columbia/Legacy), which includes appearances by Cootie Williams, Lionel Hampton, saxophonist George Auld, and Count Basie himself. The small band of pianist and singer Fats Waller was a compact swing machine (recordings on RCA/BMG), and the tightly scripted band led by bassist John Kirby also explored many avenues for interestingly arranged performances in a small-group context (Columbia/Legacy). Finally, the small bands led on recordings by several Ellingtonians, especially those of Rex Stewart and Johnny Hodges (RCA/BMG), should not be missed.

〰〰

So-called modern jazz, or bebop, at the time of World War II and just afterward, placed an increased emphasis on the soloist's ability to function coherently under very challenging conditions—especially super-fast tempos and greater density of harmonic movement. The entire group, not just the soloist, needed to be keyed to a heightened pitch of alertness and coordination.

Bebop was largely a music of small groups. Although the majority of modern-jazz performances came to be dominated by a routine in which the group would play the melody together, followed by a series of improvised solos, after which they would again play the melody and close out, many early bop recordings had interesting routines worked out for the small groups, incorporating riffs, breaks, and other compositional elements. Among these, some of the most influential were Dizzy Gillespie's 1945 small-band recordings with alto saxophone genius Charlie "Bird" Parker—"Salt Peanuts," "Groovin' High," "Shaw 'Nuff," "Dizzy Atmosphere," and several others (Guild/Musicraft originally; now available in many forms). Parker's own recordings for the small Dial label from 1946 and 1947, many of which feature young Miles Davis on trumpet, are classics of the genre and sometimes have unconventional compositional touches, especially "A Night in Tunisia," "Stupendous," "Klactoveedsedstene," "Charlie's Wig," and "Quasimodo." At the other end of the spectrum are recordings that jettison theme altogether, beginning on white-hot improvisation by Parker, especially "The Hymn" (Dial), "Bird Gets the Worm," and "Klaunstance" (Savoy).

The pianist and composer Thelonious Monk made a highly individualistic series of recordings for the Blue Note label between 1947 and 1952 with very interesting compositional elements; some of these, such as "Well You Needn't," "Evidence," and "Straight No Chaser," became jazz standards. Not to be missed is Monk's eerie 1947 orchestration of his most famous composition, "Round Midnight." Piano innovator Bud Powell's 1949 Blue Note session with trumpeter Fats Navarro and a young Sonny Rollins on tenor sax produced four classics: Powell's own "Bouncing with Bud," "Dance of the Infidels," and "Wail," along with a wild version of Monk's composition "52nd Street Theme."

Also in 1949, Miles Davis made a series of interesting and carefully planned recordings with a different kind of sound—cooler, more pensive and lyrical, perhaps, than much of the music that was being marketed as bebop at the time. These discs, which became known collectively as the Birth of the Cool recordings, also featured stars-to-be such as alto saxophonist Lee Konitz and baritone saxophonist Gerry Mulligan. The pianist and arranger Tadd Dameron also made some seminal recordings in 1947 for Blue Note with trumpeter Fats Navarro; those titles—"The Chase," "The Squirrel," "Our Delight," and "Dameronia"—are classics of orchestration and also contain thrilling solos by the short-lived trumpeter. Dameron's 1962 album *The Magic Touch* (Riverside) contains more of his marvelous writing, played by a band including pianist Bill Evans and trumpeter Clark Terry.

Musicians from the previous generation did not just disappear with the advent of bebop, of course, and some of them were extremely supportive of the new music. Foremost among these was saxophonist Coleman Hawkins, who used Dizzy Gillespie, Thelonious Monk, trumpeter Howard McGhee, and other bop luminaries on records and in live gigs as early as 1944. His 1944 Apollo recordings of "Woody'n You" and "Disorder at the Border," featuring Gillespie and drummer Max Roach, are generally thought of as being the first real bebop records. Benny Goodman used bop trumpet giant Fats Navarro and tenorist Wardell Gray on recordings, and bandleader Claude Thornhill employed many modernists. Pianist and composer Mary Lou Williams, one of the most talented and interesting orchestrators of the swing period, encouraged many of the younger players, and her Harlem apartment became a kind of salon for the likes of Bud Powell, trumpeter Kenny Dorham, Thelonious Monk, and pianist Erroll Garner.

Bop, although it was largely a small-group music, was also taken up by some big bands. The Billy Eckstine Orchestra of the early 1940s was an important incubator of the modern movement, but the two most important flat-out bop big bands were probably Dizzy Gillespie's and Woody Herman's. Herman's late-1940s recordings such as "Four Brothers," "Apple Honey," "The Goof and I," and "Early Autumn" (Columbia/Legacy) hold up very well, and feature sometimes exquisite arrangements by aces such as Ralph Burns and Al Cohn, as well as solos by saxophonists Cohn, Stan Getz, Zoot Sims, and Serge Chaloff; trumpeter Sonny Berman; and trombonist Bill Harris. Gillespie's recordings for RCA and Musicraft feature blazing virtuoso arrangements and fiery solos; "Manteca" (featuring Cuban conga drummer Chano Pozo), "Cool Breeze," "Stay on It," "Oop-Pop-A-Da," "Jumpin' with Symphony Sid" (all RCA/BMG), "Things to Come," "Emanon," and "One Bass Hit" (Musicraft) are classics.

"One Bass Hit" and the later "Two Bass Hit" (RCA/BMG) were features for bassist Ray Brown, a phenomenal technician both as soloist and as rhythm-section member, whose career lasted up into the new millennium. Bop tended to pull the rhythm section slightly more into the foreground; drummers played more aggressive commentary during others' solos, bassists took solos more regularly. All of the above-mentioned bop recordings are worth studying as examples of group playing, not just for their interesting compositional aspects. Another great bassist of that period and on through the 1950s was Oscar Pettiford, who was one of the best bop soloists regardless of instrument; he even made recordings playing jazz cello. For a taste of Pettiford's style, listen to his 1944 bass solo on "The Man I Love," recorded with Coleman Hawkins for the small Signature label and currently available on several import labels. During his very-well-recorded solo you can hear him drawing breaths between phrases, as if he were playing a horn.

The 1950s and 1960s, with the advent of long-playing records, saw an explosion in the sheer amount of jazz music recorded. Everything seemed to be up for grabs, and companies were willing to try all kinds of things to fill the record bins. It is impossible to do justice to the variety and quantity in this brief a space, but some landmarks can be pointed out.

One of the towering figures of post–World War II jazz was the bassist and composer Charles Mingus, who seemed determined to grapple with the entire jazz tradition. His great hero was Duke Ellington, and Mingus's work evinces a kindred ambition to wring variations out of the possible ways a jazz group could sound. His recordings range from stripped-down group improvisations to fully scored works for big band. A good place to start might be *Blues and Roots* (Atlantic), which contains his homage to Jelly Roll Morton, entitled "My Jelly Roll Soul"; his gospel-tinged "Wednesday Night Prayer Meeting"; and his overwhelming up-tempo riff avalanche "E's Flat, Ah's Flat, Too." The music here is planned out but also leaves space for the excellent soloists, including altoist Jackie McLean, tenorist Booker Ervin, and baritonist Pepper Adams.

Another essential Mingus recording is *Mingus Presents Mingus* (Candid), on which reedman Eric Dolphy, trumpeter Ted Curson, drummer Dannie Richmond, and Mingus himself maintain an astonishing tension between total group improvisation and certain planned-out motifs and compositional elements that thread through the music like a pattern in a carpet. The blues study "Folk Forms No. 1," the haunting and almost tempoless ballad "What Love," the gallows-humor ode to the segregationist governor of Arkansas, "Fables of Faubus," and the roiling, shifting, manic "All the Things You Could Be by Now If Sigmund Freud's Wife Was Your Mother" are some of the most adventurous and rewarding jazz performances ever recorded. Each track is a kind of essay on the balance between individual expression and the meaning of the group.

Every Mingus disc deliberately addresses this balancing act in some way, and there is no room here to discuss them all. Others to look for at the top of the list include *Mingus Dynasty, Mingus Ah Um,* and *Let My Children Hear Music* (Columbia/Legacy), *Pithecanthropus Erectus, Changes One,* and *Changes Two* (Atlantic), *Mingus at Monterey* (Prestige), and the great *Tijuana Moods* (RCA/BMG).

The Modern Jazz Quartet was a long-lived ensemble led by pianist-composer John Lewis, who constructed carefully balanced and often somewhat austere settings for himself, vibraphonist Milt

Jackson, bassist Percy Heath, and drummer Connie Kay. Their recordings are very consistent, especially those on Atlantic. Dave Brubeck was another pianist-composer who led an enormously popular quartet in the 1950s and 1960s, featuring ultracool altoist Paul Desmond. Brubeck, like John Lewis, was fascinated with the possibilities in deliberately appropriating aspects of European classical music to use with jazz. He made many recordings; the obvious place to start is *Time Out* (Columbia/Legacy), which contains the hit "Take Five." Tenor saxophonist Stan Getz recorded a very unusual album entitled *Focus* (Verve), on which arranger Eddie Sauter wrote a series of orchestrated vignettes for a string section, through which Getz was free to weave his improvised way, an interesting melding of a somewhat European classical sound with jazz improvisation.

Composer and theorist George Russell, who arranged music for Dizzy Gillespie's big band in the 1940s, likewise came up with fascinating group settings that strongly challenged soloists and had a sound all their own. His *Jazz Workshop* (RCA/BMG), *Ezzthetics* (Riverside), and *New York, N.Y.* (Decca) contain some of the most interesting compositional frameworks of the period, as well as great solo work from the likes of John Coltrane, Eric Dolphy, and Bill Evans.

As musicians experimented with new harmonic formulas, some put together groups with no piano, the idea being that a horn soloist would be less hemmed in harmonically without the piano's very specific voicings. A pioneering pianoless band was led by baritone saxophonist Gerry Mulligan; his quartet with trumpeter Chet Baker made a series of recordings for the Pacific Jazz label that contain all kinds of compositional touches and also group improvisations echoing New Orleans jazz. Tenor saxophonist Sonny

Rollins made many recordings with only bass and drum accompaniment. Among them, *A Night at the Village Vanguard*, volumes 1 and 2 (Blue Note) is an amazing example of the best kind of stream-of-consciousness jazz oratory, and *Freedom Suite* (Riverside) is a remarkable attempt in the Mingus tradition to structure a small-group performance with different compositional segments, combining improvisation with planned-out material.

Ironically, the 1950s were also a golden age of the piano trio, tightly knit ensembles of piano, bass, and drums in which piano improvisation would be closely balanced with arranged touches incorporating all three members. While there were many notable piano trios at the time, perhaps the two most influential were those led by Oscar Peterson and Bill Evans. Peterson, while not the most subtle or imaginative improviser, was an overwhelming technician, muscular and swinging, and his groups were extremely influential for their split-second, turn-on-a-dime cohesion and tidal momentum. Evans, on the other hand, was nothing if not subtle and imaginative, and his trios were intimate, chamber music–like explorations of a tune's harmonic possibilities, very lyrical usually, and with a great deal of dialogue between the piano and bass, especially.

Thelonious Monk's compositions were more than mere frameworks for improvisation; they contained rhythmic and harmonic cues that were to be taken into account during solos, and his small bands always reflected his unique musical point of view. At the center of all the music sits Monk's spiky, unorthodox piano. His album *Brilliant Corners* (Riverside), with Sonny Rollins, altoist Ernie Henry, bassist Oscar Pettiford, and drummer Max Roach, is a jazz classic. *Monk's Music* (Riverside) features a somewhat larger ensemble, including both John Coltrane and tenor saxophone patriarch Coleman Hawkins. *The Thelonious Monk Orchestra at Town*

Hall (Riverside) contains Monk compositions ingeniously scored for a full big band. And all of Monk's quartet recordings from the 1960s, especially *Straight No Chaser* and *Underground* (Columbia/Legacy) are more than worth hearing for the great cohesion of the rhythm section with tenorist Charlie Rouse.

Two other seminal bands of the period were drummer Art Blakey's Jazz Messengers and pianist Horace Silver's quintet. The cream of their work was recorded for Blue Note in the late 1950s and early 1960s. Albums such as Blakey's *Moanin'*, *The Big Beat*, and *Indestructible*, and Silver's *Doin' the Thing*, *Blowin' the Blues Away*, and *Song for My Father* present tight, cohesive, and swinging formats and a variety of rhythmic grooves. In both bands, the rhythm section plays a very aggressive, central role in the music.

Miles Davis occupies a pinnacle of his own in jazz; he may have had a more varied and flexible imagination for the possibilities in the small jazz ensemble than anyone with the exception of Charles Mingus. Highlights of his recorded work, from an ensemble standpoint, must include his quintet recordings *Relaxin'*, *Steamin'*, *Cookin'*, and *Workin'* with John Coltrane (Prestige); his sextet recordings *Milestones* and *Kind of Blue* (Columbia/Legacy), where Coltrane is joined by altoist Cannonball Adderley; the 1964 Philharmonic Hall concert, originally issued in two volumes as *Four and More* and *My Funny Valentine* (Columbia/Legacy), on which Davis shares the front line with tenor saxophonist George Coleman accompanied by the epoch-making rhythm section of Herbie Hancock, Ron Carter, and Tony Williams; and the recordings Davis made with his mid-1960s quintet, which had the Hancock-Carter-Williams rhythm section and substituted saxophonist Wayne Shorter for George Coleman. This was one of the great bands in jazz history; discs such as *ESP*, *Miles Smiles*, *Nefer-*

titi, and *Filles de Kilimanjaro* (Columbia/Legacy) are indispensable. In them, the soloists and the rhythm section are involved in a fantastic dance in which the rhythm and harmony could go through the most seemingly precarious extensions, with the members of the band still knowing exactly where they were, a real adventure of ideas and reflexes and collective storytelling. Davis's later recordings, on which he incorporated electronics and rock elements, especially the famous *Bitches Brew,* were extremely influential and laid the foundation for the so-called fusion music of the 1970s.

Mention must also be made of Davis's extremely popular and beautiful late-1950s collaborations with the orchestrator Gil Evans. Evans was one of the finest arrangers for large ensembles, and he had a special affinity for Davis's playing. Their *Miles Ahead, Porgy and Bess,* and *Sketches of Spain* are really concertos for Davis's trumpet and full orchestra, and have remained among Davis's most popular recordings. Evans's numerous recordings with his own band are also of interest to anyone with an ear for beautiful and ingenious orchestration. Especially interesting is *Great Jazz Standards* (Pacific Jazz), on which Evans reorchestrates Bix Beiderbecke's "Davenport Blues," Don Redman's "Chant of the Weed," and a number of other earlier compositions.

The 1960s also saw a wholesale reexamination of the rhythmic, harmonic, and ensemble ground rules that had characterized jazz for decades. From an ensemble perspective, the 1960s avant-garde seemed in large measure to be about the breaking down of boundaries between foreground and background elements. The drums and bass, especially, were encouraged to be full constituent members of the front line, along with the horns. In a way, this development represented an attempt to retrieve some of the spirit of collective improvisation of the New Orleans ensemble.

The two most influential figures of the 1960s jazz avant-garde were indisputably the saxophonist/bandleaders Ornette Coleman and John Coltrane. Both tried to expand the canvas of jazz beyond the language inherited from Charlie Parker, and both worked out distinctive and original ensemble concepts. Coltrane had come up in the bebop era and played in bands led by Dizzy Gillespie and Johnny Hodges, among others. His language on the tenor saxophone was rooted in the language of older players such as Coleman Hawkins, Don Byas, Sonny Stitt, and Charlie Parker, but his ear led him to listen beyond that language in many ways. From an ensemble standpoint, his most important group was doubtless the quartet he assembled in the very early 1960s with pianist McCoy Tyner, bassist Jimmy Garrison, and drummer Elvin Jones. The albums they made for the Impulse label, especially *A Love Supreme*, *Crescent*, *Coltrane*, and *Coltrane Live at Birdland*, showed a phenomenally adventuresome ensemble in which each member was a fully participating element of an ever evolving group counterpoint. They ran the range from exquisite lyricism to extraordinary, exhilarating polyrhythmic explorations; drummer Elvin Jones, particularly, maintained an ongoing dialogue with the leader that must be heard to be believed. Coltrane made several records toward the end of his life (he died at the age of forty in 1967) with larger ensembles in which nearly everyone was playing in full cry, constantly, without the usual rhythmic and harmonic conventions. *Meditations* and, especially, *Ascension* (Impulse) are shocking for most listeners to encounter, even today; they are without parallel for emotionally draining intensity.

~~~

Ornette Coleman's playing experience had been rooted largely in a rhythm-and-blues background, but his grasp of the essential truths of jazz was profound. His pianoless quartet of the early 1960s, with trumpeter Don Cherry, bassist Charlie Haden, and either Ed Blackwell or Billy Higgins on drums, caused a sensation. Coleman claimed to want to dispense with conventional harmony, rhythmic expectations, and ensemble roles, and he did this to a large extent while still making music that swung and was emotionally accessible. He loved to put the bass or the drums in the forefront, and to undercut the listener's expectations of what a jazz group should do. Albums such as *Change of the Century, This Is Our Music,* and especially *The Shape of Jazz to Come* (Atlantic) sound extremely fresh today, and show an ensemble full of brilliant individuals working to redefine for themselves, yet again, what jazz means. Coleman's "double quartet" album *Free Jazz* (Atlantic) is discussed earlier; also essential to understanding Coleman are the two volumes of *At the Golden Circle* (Blue Note) and *Town Hall, 1962* (ESP), which feature Coleman with a trio including bassist David Izenzon and drummer Charles Moffett.

The 1960s avant-garde produced many recordings that challenge some conceptions of what jazz is all about. Debate still goes on concerning the merits of some musicians allied with that movement, but certainly anyone who would understand jazz needs to listen and make up his or her own mind. Nobody questions the virtuosity and seriousness of pianist Cecil Taylor, a musician of prodigious gifts who has refused to compromise his own vision of music, often abandoning the regular tempos and harmonic and rhythmic cues that underlie most jazz. His discs *Unit Structures* and *Conquistador* (Blue Note) show his unique compositional and performing approach.

Tenor saxophonist Albert Ayler is a favorite of fans of the 1960s avant-garde. He was a fiery player who wrung all kinds of extreme and unusual sonorities out of the horn, and led groups in which each member enjoyed a high degree of independence. His discs *Spirits Rejoice* and *Spiritual Unity* (ESP) show his intense approach at its peak. Chicago saxophonist Roscoe Mitchell's *Sound* (Delmark) took the "freedom principle" (critic John Litweiler's phrase) just about as far as it could be taken, and much of the time, each of the various musicians assembled in the studio seemed to be going about his own business oblivious of the others.

At the same time that the avant-garde players were following their path, many players had arrived who stopped short of abandoning harmony and rhythm but were looking for something beyond the conventional setup of melody, series of solos, melody, and then closeout. One important and overlooked composer and bandleader at that time was pianist Andrew Hill, whose Blue Note albums, especially *Point of Departure* and *Black Fire,* should have been more influential than they were. One of his musical companions was tenor saxophonist Joe Henderson, who made a number of records on which the ensemble achieved a high level of suppleness and freshness, especially *Mode for Joe* and *Our Thing* (Blue Note). Altoist Jackie McLean, who grew up on the language of Charlie Parker, blossomed as a bandleader and composer during the 1960s; his discs *Capuchin Swing, A Fickle Sonance, Jackie's Bag, New Soil, Let Freedom Ring,* and *One Step Beyond* are landmarks of the era, melding elements of the avant-garde with the bebop language.

At the end of this list, I must repeat the disclaimer offered at its start: This is no more than a brief list, with many omissions. For more detailed and extensive and comprehensive listening suggestions, *The Penguin Guide to Jazz* (Penguin) and this author's *The Guide to Classic Recorded Jazz* (University of Iowa Press) are recommended.

Lester Young, Walter Page, Jimmy Rushing, Count Basie, and fans. Photograph *courtesy of the Duncan Scheidt Collection.*

Two

Blues

"Blues" is a word with several meanings in jazz. It refers both to a specific song form and also to a body of expressive techniques that may be used in any kind of material, regardless of form. Beyond that, it refers to a stance, a way of approaching experience, including the experience of playing music.

Jazz came into being from a stew of many elements—marching-band music, light classical music, opera, nineteenth-century parlor songs, French and Spanish music, as well as the blues—in New Orleans especially, about a hundred years ago. Some critics argue that all these elements were, and are, equally important or basic to jazz. But of all these elements, the blues form is the only one that has been explored by musicians of every style and era in jazz; it has occupied a place at the center of the music from the beginning. In fact, one side of the first jazz record ever made was the "Livery Stable Blues," recorded in 1917 by the Original Dixieland Jazz Band, a group from New Orleans.

Originally the property of African American laborers and itinerant troubadours in the rural American South, the blues form became standardized as it began to get written down and published early in the twentieth century, initially through the pioneering efforts of the bandleader and composer W. C. Handy. Handy composed blues songs that became standards in jazz and American popular music, including "St. Louis Blues," "Memphis Blues," "Hesitation Blues," and many others. Partly fueled by the success of Handy's compositions, the blues became a popular musical craze for a time in the late teens and the twenties, as ragtime had been several years previously. And it was the extraordinary success of a recording of a blues song—"Crazy Blues," by the African American popular singer Mamie Smith in 1920—that opened the doors wide to African American recording artists of all types in the 1920s.

The blues has been played by King Oliver, Jelly Roll Morton, Louis Armstrong, Benny Goodman, Bix Beiderbecke, Jack Teagarden, Mary Lou Williams, Duke Ellington, Art Tatum, Fats Waller, Count Basie, Woody Herman, Coleman Hawkins, Lester Young, Charlie Parker, Dizzy Gillespie, Miles Davis, Stan Getz, Charles Mingus, Ornette Coleman, Eric Dolphy, Thelonious Monk, John Coltrane, and more or less every other jazz musician that one can think of. It is not just one among many other elements, as, say, marching-band music was. It has remained vital and central to jazz, throughout all of jazz's eras and stylistic permutations. Even in the most musically sophisticated performances, the blues reaches back to an earlier, less urban, more earthy element, a cry, a rasp, a shout. As a form, it is the lingua franca of jazz—for most of jazz's history, it has been a starting point, a place for musicians to warm up and get to know one another, a shared body of text and language. But what is the blues?

It may be helpful to see the blues as a huge river running through the center of our culture. Almost every notable form of American music in the twentieth century is a city, or a village, along that river. Jazz, rock and roll, rhythm and blues, bluegrass, and even so-called serious music (modern music in the European classical tradition) have all drawn strength, power, and refreshment from, and owe much of their character to, the blues. The blues has been played and sung by lone men and women with guitars and by full orchestras, by jug bands, rock-and-roll groups, jazz pianists, and cabaret singers. The blues' borders are porous, and its influence has seeped out into nearly everything surrounding it.

Formally, the blues most commonly consists of a line, a kind of proposition, which is then repeated over a slightly altered harmonic background. Then a rhymed, answering third line arrives, and the effect is satisfying. When jazz musicians say, "Let's play some blues," they are almost always referring to this form. In musical terms, one trip through this form usually lasts for 12 measures (or "bars"), and that little 12-bar cycle is played over and over until the musicians decide to stop. Each time through this 12-bar form is called a "chorus." The form can be played in any tempo—slow, medium, or fast.

For a good example, listen to track 2, "Boogie Woogie," recorded in 1936 by a small contingent from the Count Basie band, including Count Basie himself on piano, tenor saxophonist Lester Young, trumpeter Carl Smith, bassist Walter Page, drummer Jo Jones, and one of the great blues singers, Jimmy Rushing.

To get an immediate feel for the structure of the blues, proceed directly to Rushing's first vocal chorus, beginning at about the 0:31 mark. It is, formally, a perfect example of the blues' construction. Rushing sings the first line—"Wanna see my baby, see my baby bad"—then repeats it almost exactly over a slightly altered harmonic background. Then he delivers the third, rhyming, line—"That's the sweetest woman that I've ever had"—and there you have the basic unit of currency of the blues. A statement of a desire, a tension, a question, a problem, or an observation, which is then restated, and then balanced or answered or extended with a (usually) rhymed third line. In other words, a thought, a slightly altered restatement of the thought, and then a third, answering thought.

After this first chorus, Rushing sings three more choruses, each with the same structure. In principle, and if there were room on the record, Rushing could go on singing choruses ad infinitum; they are modular, like links on a chain or the floors of a skyscraper. Each of these brief choruses contains within it the organic principle of the buildup and release of tension, a tiny model of beginning, middle, and end. When the musicians play their solos, beginning with saxophonist Lester Young's entrance after Rushing's vocal (at about 1:35), they are playing over this same repeated, modular 12-bar form.

And although in chapter 4 we will look in some detail at the raw materials the musicians use to improvise their variations, it may be worth knowing now that there are standard harmonic relations between the three "thoughts" mentioned above. While almost always altered and varied, the basic template is this: The first thought, lasting the first four bars, is pitched in the home key of the piece; the second thought, lasting the second four bars, travels out to a different key and then returns home; the third thought, lasting for the final four bars of the form, goes to yet another key center, where a harmonic tension is set up that pulls us, finally, back to the home key, where we are then ready to go around again for another chorus. Rarely, though, is this set of harmonic relationships found in such a simple form; this is the most basic way of putting the relationships, and it has been subjected to countless variations throughout jazz's history. The blues may be played in all tempos, moods, and orchestrations, but it always has this same quality of compressed cycles of beginning, middle, and end.

The other track on the accompanying CD that is a blues in form is "Footprints" (track 6), recorded by the Miles Davis Quintet thirty years after "Boogie Woogie." On the surface, the two tracks might seem as different as could be, but if you listen closely to "Footprints," you will hear the blues form played over and over.

Ron Carter's bass sets the stage alone, playing a repeated, rising phrase that continues throughout the track. He is joined quickly by Herbie Hancock's piano and Tony Williams's drums, and these three instruments play a kind of prologue until the entry of the horns and the formal beginning of the tune. This occurs at 0:20, when Miles Davis's trumpet and Wayne Shorter's saxophone enter playing the chantlike theme.

Listen to the first chorus. Over that repeated bass figure, you'll hear Davis and Shorter play a first "thought" (0:20), consisting of a linked rising and falling phrase. Beginning at 0:28, they repeat this thought, over the same background, altering it slightly and tacking on an extra, descending, phrase. Then, at 0:36, they play a third thought, beginning similarly to the other two and consisting of brief, linked phrases. They begin a new chorus at 0:44, repeating this melody. The three thoughts that make up a full chorus of the melody are similar, formally, to the three parts of Jimmy Rushing's choruses on "Boogie Woogie"—a line, then the same line (almost) repeated, and then a kind of punch line . . . and then it begins again.

Notice that each time the musicians arrive at the third thought in "Footprints," the background shifts; the bass suddenly begins playing a series of very quick notes instead of the repeated phrase. As they finish the third thought, the bass shifts back to the original repeated phrase. Every time they go through this form, the background will shift in a noticeable way when they get to the third part; if you lose your place in the form, focus your attention on what the bass is doing and you will get reoriented.

And, as in "Boogie Woogie," the performance as a whole consists of a series of variations played over this short, repeated form. It is more challenging to hear the chorus structure here because the rhythm section is playing around with the tempo and the rhythms so brilliantly. But if you pay attention to what the bass is playing, that will usually clue you in to the place where the third thought enters, and ends, beginning a new chorus.

~~~

In addition, though, beyond just the form, the blues involves certain characteristic expressive elements. Listen, for example, to the way Rushing hollers, "Baaaayyy-by what's on your worried mind" in "Boogie Woogie"—the way the notes arch and bend, a call for a response. Or to Wayne Shorter's tenor saxophone from 5:50 to 6:00 of "Footprints." This kind of crying out, this bending or smearing of notes, has been a central part of jazz musicians' expressive palettes from the beginning. It is a technique rooted in the blues, but jazz musicians don't use it exclusively on the blues.

They apply it to all kinds of material, and it amounts to a way of appropriating the material—turning it, in a real sense, into jazz.

This technique, or expressive tendency, usually involves two different elements. One is the alteration of the expected notes of the scale in which the musician would seem to be playing, and the other is the alteration of the actual sound quality of the note as played. We can look at these two elements separately, even though they are intimately related. Readers with no musical training will have to forgive a small amount of technical discussion in this section.

The first element, that of altering the given musical scale, involves using what have commonly been called "blue notes"— most typically the flatted third and seventh notes of the major scale. For instance, in a C-major scale, the third note, E, and the leading tone, B, would be flatted, to E-flat and B-flat, respectively. This tendency to bend or alter these particular notes makes some listeners think that the blues have a minor-key cast to them, but this is normally not the case.

What the alteration, which is usually only temporary, does is introduce a discord into the proceedings—not a pointless discord but one that creates a very pointed tension, a reminder that things are not necessarily the way they seem on the surface. Sometimes these discords resolve, and sometimes they linger. Sometimes they arise on the way to the note that will resolve them, and sometimes they are themselves the point, and they remain, like a question mark. The more complex the tune, the more complex will be the network of harmonic interrelationships. What is a discord in one measure of music may not be discordant a few measures down the road.

We can hear an instructive example on "The Eternal Triangle" (track 7). "The Eternal Triangle" is not a blues in structure, but the playing of the musicians is full of these other blues techniques. Around the 5:53 mark, tenor saxophonist Sonny Stitt is coming to the end of a chorus (there are "choruses" in the majority of jazz forms, not just in blues, as you will see in chapter 3) and is about to begin another, when he ends a phrase with a very significant note—a D-flat that hangs there for a brief moment before Stitt starts repeating it as the beginning note of a new chorus. What is he doing?

Overall, "The Eternal Triangle" is set in the key of B-flat, and that note, D-flat, is the flatted third (the normal third is D) of the B-flat major scale—a blue note. But Stitt plays it, initially, at a point where the background harmony happens to be an F dominant 7 chord. In that context, the D-flat functions as the raised fifth note (C-sharp, which is the same tone as D-flat, just with a different name) of the F-major scale. In other words, it first occurs to Stitt to play the D-flat in order to imply an F augmented chord, which is an acceptable substitute for the F dominant 7.

But when the new chorus begins, the harmony shifts back to the home chord of B-flat major, and the meaning of that D-flat changes—it suddenly becomes the "blue" flatted third in the B-flat major scale. Hearing it, Stitt thinks, "All right, I'll play some blues," and he hangs on that D-flat for half of his very bluesy first eight bars; in his second eight, beginning at 6:01, he decides to continue that line of thought and does some blues shouting and preaching with a little series of ascending phrases. Jazz musicians, it is worth saying, listen not just to what the others in the group are playing, but to what they themselves are playing, and they have to be alive to the implications of things they have just said; surprises and opportunities arise often without the musicians anticipating them. But the players need to be knowledge-able, coordinated, and quick-witted enough to be able to use them on a moment's notice.

Of course, the technique of setting up passing discords to create tensions that resolve is hardly unique to jazz music. Bach did it, Beethoven practically made his name doing it, and when we get to the Romantic era of European music, it seems to move from being a part of the expressive vocabulary to being almost the entire point. Twentieth-century European music is full of discords that do not resolve at all, and harmonic landscapes where any notion of "resolution" is nonexistent, such as the 12-tone system. But the specific notes that jazz musicians choose for their discords, and the way they function musically, are a big part of what makes jazz identifiable. In any case, for most of jazz's history, the music has depended to a large degree on this creating and dispelling of tension by means of "blue" and other discordant notes.

~~~

Hand in hand with this tendency goes a disposition toward altering notes not just harmonically but timbrally—a musicologist might say "vocalizing" them. Rather than striving for a Platonic purity of tone, an ideal sound, as a classical orchestral musician might, every jazz musician strives to develop a personal sound, one that is unique and that expresses his or her own personality and sensibility. Partly this involves the alteration of the sounds of notes; a given note may be played with a range of different timbral effects. Jazz musicians achieve this by all kinds of means—for example, by using different types of mutes for brass players, by making growls in the throat while playing a note, and by playing so-called alternate fingerings on the woodwinds.

Again, this disposition is not unique to jazz music. It is found throughout almost every type of non-Western music—certainly throughout African music of all types, classical music of India, Native American music, Middle Eastern music, and so on. We may think of European classical musicians as striving for a certain purity and evenness of tone, but in the music of composers like Bartók, Shostakovich, and many other twentieth-century figures, the instruments, especially the strings, are presented with a range of tone-altering instructions, including to play with the wooden back of the bow instead of the hairs, to play harmonies (lightly touching the string without pressing it down), or hitting the strings.

When jazz musicians employ comparable techniques, it is often to create a specifically vocal effect, as if the note were being sung. One common technique is the manipulation of a rubber plunger mute—a simple rubber bathroom plunger—over the bell of a brass instrument. This manipulation allows the player to change the quality of a note as it is played, as the movement of a speaker's lips alters the sounds of syllables as they are spoken. Trumpeter Carl Smith does it very subtly in his solo on "Boogie Woogie." You can hear Duke Ellington's entire trombone section doing it on "U.M.M.G."; when the saxophones enter playing the theme, at 1:33, listen to the brass choir behind them. They achieve that "boo-wah" figure by first slightly blocking the horn's bell with the rubber plunger, and then removing it.

Other instruments achieve similar effects in various ways; for one example, listen to the very vocalized clarinet break at 2:18 of King Oliver's "Weather Bird Rag." Sonny Rollins loves to do this kind of thing; listen to the series of descending figures he plays in

"Moritat" at 2:23, or listen at 3:02, when he alludes to the melody, or to the little grunt he emits at 3:42, or the yelp of assent right around 5:43, during his exchanges with drummer Max Roach. Stan Getz does it in his own way, to a somewhat different effect, throughout "I Can't Get Started." Listen to the salty little phrase he plays at 2:27, and the blues phrases he barks out at around 3:25. Many of the things Miles Davis does without a mute in his trumpet solo on "Footprints" have this same vocalized quality; for a clear example, listen to what he plays between 3:00 and 3:30.

And for a short anthology of all these techniques, listen to Dizzy Gillespie's trumpet solo in "The Eternal Triangle." He begins his second chorus, at 9:20, with very bluesy phrases; at 9:28 he repeats a humorous vocalized figure that he achieves by manipulating the valves in an unorthodox way. The entire first 16 bars of his next chorus, beginning at 9:46 and going to 9:59, consist of blues phrases using the flatted third and seventh of the B-flat scale, as well as timbrally altered notes.

The point isn't to show every instance in which the language and techniques of the blues appear in these performances, only to show that this sensibility is found in jazz not only in performances of material in the blues form. It is a blues-based sensibility that shapes jazz expression across the board, regardless of the material being played, and it is one of the elements that marks jazz as jazz.

This blues disposition is also found in most other American musics in varying degrees. Country music has been strongly inflected by the blues since its earliest days, when the Carter Family and, especially, Jimmie Rodgers recorded significant amounts of blues material; Rodgers even recorded one of his trademark yodeling blues with Louis Armstrong accompanying him. Bluegrass pioneer Bill Monroe was clearly deeply influenced by blues and by early experiences playing with a black guitarist in Rosine, Kentucky; many of the syncopations and timbral inflections that came to mark bluegrass clearly come from the blues. Hank Williams, who took informal early lessons from a black street singer, recorded many blues songs. Cajun music is also full of blues techniques and forms. Early performers such as accordionist Amedee Ardoin and singer-guitarist Cleoma Breaux Falcon put the blues at the center of their repertoire, and the fact that they sung it in French did nothing to lessen the impact of its message.

When we come to rock and roll, the influence is obvious. Chuck Berry, Elvis Presley, Little Richard, Ray Charles, and most of the other early rock-and-roll heroes based much of their repertoire and style on earlier blues and rhythm-and-blues performers. And, of course, rock guitar heroes in the mold of Jimi Hendrix, Eric Clapton, and Jimmy Page achieved many of their most characteristic effects by finding ways of timbrally altering and distorting the notes they were playing, and that disposition goes straight back to the blues.

~~~

Beyond these technical or quantifiable elements, the blues implies, as stated earlier, a certain type of stance. There is something bittersweet and self-contradictory in the blues; it is a way of expressing paradox, of saying two things at the same time. "You keep me worried and bothered all the time," Jimmy Rushing sings, in a jolly enough voice, as the band swings away underneath him. This is not just a form of psychic dissociation; it is a way of neutralizing the harder facts of life, or at least reducing them to manageable size, by insisting on confronting them with grace, wit, and resilience.

Of course, one can look at it from the other side as well: The blues is also a way of reminding us, in the middle of our party, our dance, that hard times are a fact of life, too, and not to take our good times for granted. The blues fuses, in a sense, the comic and the tragic views of life. Depending on the individual musician's sensibility, these different angles will be mixed in different degrees, but they will always be mixed in some way, and this mixture of modes is central to most American artistic expression, not only to jazz. In American literature, one might think of the difference between Mark Twain and Herman Melville—both writers mixed tragic and comic modes, although Twain clearly felt closer to the comic mode and Melville to the tragic. You will find the same spectrum of sensibility among jazz's musicians.

In both the blues on this disc, to speak only of the blues, as different as they are, there is this double sensibility at work, this inherent duality or ambivalence. In "Boogie Woogie," one might say things are a little closer to the optimism-in-the-midst-of-bad-news end of things; a community that supports each individual story with buoyant continuity and a danceable ground rhythm that continues on and on, constantly moving forward, a series of rhythmic and harmonic variations on an agreed-upon group idea. The soloists set up constant tensions with the underlying rhythms and harmonies, and then ingeniously resolve them in the nick of time. Some of the same remarks might apply to "Footprints," but how different the mood is here. The drums are explosive and even celebratory, but the underlying harmony is itself ambiguous and unresolved, and the background rhythm keeps shifting too; the musicians are dancing in the midst of uncertainty—definitely a blues attitude.

And, ultimately, that improvisatory stance, that willingness to incorporate tension and uncertainty into the aesthetic rather than eliminate or minimize them, the willingness to make the process itself part of the art, even to accept imperfection itself as an integral part of that process, is a large part of why some feel that jazz is not just an art form but a way of living in the world.

Further Listening:

Blues

The blues is the form to which jazz musicians have returned more than any other; in it, they have found an astonishing variety of inspiration. It would be impossible, and in any case pointless, to list all the blues-based jazz records worth hearing, but here is a listing of either classic and essential statements in the form, or records that have something else extraordinary to recommend them.

To hear the blues in its most immediate form, to hear those expressive qualities in their original habitat, in a sense, it is important to have some acquaintance at least with the country-blues performers who kept alive the blues' roots in rural southern African American life. Probably the best all-around introduction to the blues in all its shadings and variety is the Grammy Award–winning five-CD set *Martin Scorsese Presents the Blues: A Musical Journey*, which contains tracks not only from pioneers such as Charley Patton, Blind Lemon Jefferson, and Blind Willie McTell but also from later proponents such as Sonny Boy Williamson, Muddy Waters, and others up to the present day.

The Dallas street singer Blind Lemon Jefferson was the first country-blues recording star, and his late-1920s records contain vocals that hark back to field hollers and work songs, as well as imaginative guitar work. His recordings, and the singing and guitar playing of Charley Patton, Son House, Skip James, and the other Mississippi Delta blues singers of the 1920s and their slightly younger follower Robert Johnson, will tell you what you need to know about the roots of the blues. Jefferson, Patton, House, and James made their early recordings for the long-defunct Paramount label, and they are available today in many forms; you will find the best sound quality on the Yazoo label, although be warned that the sound, transferred from extremely rare old 78-rpm records, is still noisy. But don't let that stop you. The two volumes of *Robert Johnson: King of the Delta Blues Singers* (Columbia/Legacy) contain some of the most powerful and influential blues ever recorded, and the sound quality is generally quite good.

Most of the early New Orleans jazz masters were strong blues players. The first jazz record, from 1917, was "Livery Stable Blues," by the Original Dixieland Jazz Band (RCA/BMG), and is worth hearing for its terrific brio and sense of fun. This was the music that announced jazz to the world at large. The King Oliver Creole Jazz Band made many great blues recordings, beginning with their first record in 1923, one side of which was "Canal Street Blues." Other landmark blues recordings by this band include "Dippermouth Blues," with its famous cornet solo by Oliver, and "Chimes Blues," which contains the first recorded solo by Louis Armstrong. These recordings are available in many forms; the best presentation and sound may be found on the Retrieval label, from England.

When Louis Armstrong began recording as a leader in his own right, in 1926, some of his best and most classic work was done on the blues. Taken together, the Hot Five and Hot Seven recordings are among the most important in jazz. Nobody should miss hearing his searingly intense solos on "S.O.L. Blues" and "Muggles," his quiet and subtly melodic solo on "Savoy Blues," and his masterpiece "West End Blues" (Columbia/Legacy). Armstrong also made recordings accompanying a number of the classic blues singers of that time, most notably Bessie Smith; standout titles with Smith include "St. Louis Blues," "Cold in Hand Blues," and "J. C. Holmes Blues" (Columbia/Legacy). He also recorded several sides with the great Ma Rainey, including the original version of the classic "See See Rider," available on a number of imported labels.

Bessie Smith, Ma Rainey, and the other "classic blues singers" with roots in the African American vaudeville tradition made many records with jazz accompaniment, often provided by members of the Fletcher Henderson Orchestra. Other blues singers of that time who received notable jazz accompaniments include Ida Cox, Sippie Wallace, Clara Smith, Trixie Smith, and Sara Martin. Their recordings are available today, for the most part, in scattershot form, although the British label Document has issued everything they recorded in wildly variable sound quality, on discs intended mainly for serious collectors. Document has also issued complete editions of everything by the above-mentioned country-blues singers and, apparently, every other pre–World War II blues performer, a staggering fact. You may search their catalog online at www.document-records.com. But in general, unless you are a completist, the Yazoo issues of this material are to be much preferred for their superior sound quality.

The pioneering jazz composer Jelly Roll Morton found many ways of handling the blues in his late-1920s recordings with his Red Hot Peppers, always imaginative and containing interesting orchestrational touches. Important examples include "Dead Man Blues," "Sidewalk Blues," and "Jungle Blues" (RCA/BMG). Morton was also a good blues singer; his famous 1939 recording of "Mamie's Blues" (Commodore) has an unforgettable mood. But all of Morton's performances, so close to the roots of jazz, are deeply pervaded by a blues sensibility. Anyone with a taste for the New Orleans style of clarinet will want to hear four other classic performances: Johnny Dodds's "Perdido Street Blues" (Columbia/Legacy), Leon Rappolo's solo on the New Orleans Rhythm Kings' "Tin Roof Blues" (recorded originally for Gennett; available on imported labels), George Lewis's "Burgundy Street Blues," and Sidney Bechet's "Blue Horizon" (Blue Note).

Many of the younger Chicago followers of the New Orleans players were excellent blues players. Foremost was cornetist Muggsy Spanier, a master of the plunger mute, who was deeply inspired by King Oliver. Early recordings such as "Bull Frog Blues" (with the Charles Pierce Orchestra) and "Friars' Point Shuffle" (with the Jungle Kings) are classics (available in various imported forms, especially on JSP, from England); both include fabulous blues playing by the short-lived clarinetist Frank Teschemacher. Spanier's most famous blues performance was probably the 1939 "Relaxin' at the Touro," with his own Ragtime Band (RCA/BMG).

Another blues specialist associated with the Chicago school was Texas trombonist and singer Jack Teagarden; his early recordings "Makin' Friends" (Columbia/Legacy) and "That's a Serious Thing" (RCA/BMG), both recorded with groups led by guitarist and impresario Eddie Condon, are blues standouts. "Beale St. Blues," by a small 1931 band led by violinist Joe Venuti and guitarist Eddie Lang and including Teagarden and Benny Goodman, is not to be missed (Decca/GRP).

Most big bands had at least several pieces in their repertoire that were based on the blues form, but several bands specialized in the blues—above all, that of Count Basie. The band's first big hit was the blues "One O'Clock Jump," followed by characteristic performances like "Swingin' the Blues," "Blues in the Dark," "Good

Morning Blues," "Sent for You Yesterday" (Decca), "Goin' to Chicago," and "Harvard Blues" (Columbia/Legacy). The Kansas City Six, a small group from the Count Basie band, made a couple of classic blues records in 1938—"Countless Blues" and "Pagin' the Devil" (Commodore)—featuring saxophonist Lester Young in two of his rare and precious appearances playing clarinet. Pianist Jay McShann, whose band, like Basie's, started in Kansas City, was also a blues specialist; his early 1940s recordings are classic big-band blues, especially "Hootie Blues" and "Jumpin' the Blues" (Decca), both of which contain terrific alto sax solos by the very young Charlie Parker. The English label Proper has put out a two-disc collection of McShann recordings entitled *Jumpin' the Blues,* which includes these as well as a number of rare and excellent small-band sides featuring the band's singer, Walter Brown.

Duke Ellington did more with the blues—found more ways to play them, more ingenious ways to disguise them—than any other single figure in jazz. Again, it would be impossible here to delve into a complete résumé of Ellington's work in the blues form, but some landmark examples are necessary. "Black and Tan Fantasy," which he recorded many times over the course of his fifty-year recording career, is a multipart composition, one section of which is a 12-bar blues played by one of Ellington's growl-specialist trumpeters, most notably Bubber Miley and Cootie Williams. A particularly great and well-recorded version may be heard on *The Popular Duke Ellington* (RCA/BMG), from 1966. "KoKo," "Across the Track Blues," "Main Stem," and "Happy-Go-Lucky Local" (RCA/BMG) are among his best pre–World War II blues orchestrations. "St. Louis Blues," recorded live at a 1940 concert in Fargo, North Dakota (Vintage Jazz Classics), is a roaring and uninhibited performance that contains a buoyant vocal from Ivie Anderson and incendiary solos from tenor saxophonist Ben Webster and trombonist Tricky Sam Nanton en route to a wild and cataclysmic finale, in which the band quotes satirically from George Gershwin's "Rhapsody in Blue."

"Diminuendo and Crescendo in Blue," from the 1956 *Ellington at Newport* (Columbia/Legacy), is a revisitation of a two-part Ellington composition originally recorded in 1937. This live performance is remarkable for the legendary extended tenor saxophone solo that Paul Gonsalves plays at the tune's midpoint; he peels off no fewer than twenty-seven choruses of rocking blues tenor and came close to starting a riot. This is one of the most famous recordings in jazz history, essential for any collection. "Ad Lib on Nippon," from the 1966 *Far East Suite* (RCA/BMG), is an extremely interesting performance heavily featuring Ellington's piano; one can listen to it several times before realizing that it is, in fact, a well-disguised blues.

Many small-group recordings were made by members of the Ellington orchestra through the decades; one of the best, from a blues or any other standpoint, is a 1940 session under the leadership of trumpeter Rex Stewart, which produced, among other excellent tracks, "Mobile Bay" and "Poor Bubber" (RCA/BMG), two sides that show a fantastic range of deep blues sonority on the trumpet. A 1940 duet between Ellington's piano and the short-lived but profoundly influential bass phenomenon Jimmy Blanton, entitled "Mr. J. B. Blues" (RCA/BMG), is a classic performance. Lastly, a one-time-only trio of Ellington, bassist Charles Mingus, and drummer Max Roach recorded the very unusual "Backward Country Boy Blues" for the album *Money Jungle* (Blue Note).

Boogie-woogie became a craze in the late 1930s, although this pulsating, danceable way of playing the blues, usually on the piano, stretches back at least into the 1920s. Meade Lux Lewis's "Honky Tonk Train Blues," which he recorded several times for various labels, is one of the archetypal boogie performances. Pianists Pete Johnson and Albert Ammons recorded separately, sometimes in a duet, and occasionally in a three-piano group with Meade Lux Lewis. Some of their duets, along with a version of "Honky Tonk Train" and a number of solos by the great blues pianist Jimmy Yancey, may still be found on the disc *Barrelhouse Boogie* (RCA/BMG). Another essential boogie-woogie performance is Pete Johnson's duet with Kansas City blues shouter Joe Turner on "Roll 'Em Pete" (Columbia/Legacy).

Big bands also jumped in on the boogie fad; Mary Lou Williams's arrangement of "Roll 'Em" was played by several, notably that of Benny Goodman (Columbia/Legacy). Another justly famous big-band boogie performance was from the band led by pianist Earl Hines, entitled "Boogie-Woogie on the St. Louis Blues" (RCA/BMG). And while not really a boogie-woogie, the Erskine Hawkins Orchestra's recording of the slow blues "After Hours" (RCA/BMG), with low-down piano by Avery Parrish, was right in the piano-blues pocket that the boogie-woogie players loved when they slowed things down. By the way, at the same session that produced the track "The Eternal Triangle," Dizzy Gillespie, Sonny Rollins, and Sonny Stitt did an extended remake of "After Hours," with pianist Ray Bryant doing a fine Avery Parrish impersonation. It can be found on Gillespie's disc *Sonny Side Up* (Verve).

In the 1940s, blues remained the lingua franca of jazz through the experiments of the bebop era. Charlie Parker, in particular, was one of the great blues players in the history of jazz, and wrote many blues lines that demonstrated the almost infinite variety available in the form, many of which became jazz standards. "Now's the Time," "Parker's Mood," "Billie's Bounce," "Barbados," "Cheryl," "Another Hair-Do," "Buzzy," "Sippin' at Bell's" (Savoy), "Big Foot," "Cool Blues," "Relaxin' at Camarillo" (Dial), "Au Privave," "Chi-Chi," "Blues for Alice," and "Visa" (Verve) are just some of the best known of the blues that came from his fertile imagination. In 1945 he participated, with his fellow pioneer Dizzy Gillespie, in a recording session for the tiny Comet label under the leadership of vibraphonist Red Norvo and recorded multiple takes of the fast "Congo Blues" and the slow "Slam Slam Blues," both great performances (currently available on Stash). And in 1952 Parker participated in a studio jam session next to alto saxophonists Johnny Hodges and Benny Carter and tenorist Ben Webster, which included the slow "Funky Blues" and the fast "Jam Blues" (Verve). Parker's hero Lester Young was a great blues player as well, and he made at least four classic blues recordings in the late 1940s: "DB Blues," "No Eyes Blues" (Aladdin), "Back to the Land," and "Up 'N Adam" (Verve). The father of the jazz tenor saxophone, Coleman Hawkins, not notable as a great blues player in his youth, became one of the great ones in his middle age. A little-known 1949 Hawkins masterpiece, recorded in France for Vogue Records, is called "Sih-Sah," and is one of the most intense blues instrumentals ever committed to disc.

The huge increase in the amount of music that was recorded due to the advent of the long-playing record makes it almost impossible to mount a reasonable survey in a short space. One points to highlights, but only with the certainty that many examples, just as good or better, will present themselves on further reflection.

Still, some performances must be singled out. We can start by mentioning several classic albums devoted to blues. *Louis Arm-*

strong Plays W. C. Handy (Columbia/Legacy) is one of the best records Armstrong ever made; with his small band, he plays a series of compositions by the man who first wrote down the blues and made it a commercial form, including "St. Louis Blues," "Memphis Blues," "Beale Street Blues," and a number of others. Armstrong's trumpet and his vocal phrasing are at their 1950s peak, and this is a record full of deep feeling and subtle profundity. *Coltrane Plays the Blues* (Atlantic) has tenor giant John Coltrane playing several different flavors of blues, and is one of the neglected highlights of Trane's catalog of recordings. The same remarks apply to *Bluesnik* by alto saxophonist Jackie McLean (Blue Note), a set of ingeniously varied blues by one of Charlie Parker's most talented and individualistic disciples. *Blues and Roots* by Charles Mingus (Atlantic) is one of the best jazz albums ever recorded; few of the tracks are formally 12-bar blues, but all the compositions are drenched in blues techniques. Worthy of special note is the volcanic fast blues "E's Flat, Ah's Flat, Too." *Red in Bluesville* (Prestige) is a mostly mellow album by Red Garland, who was Miles Davis's pianist at the time. Garland had his limitations, but playing the blues wasn't one of them. Pianist Ray Bryant's *Alone with the Blues* (Prestige) is an excellent solo effort from an unjustly neglected talent.

From among the almost countless individual blues performances on recordings from the 1950s and 1960s, here are some landmark moments. We may as well start with Miles Davis, who recorded more blues in more interesting varieties, perhaps, than any other leader in that period with the exception of Duke Ellington. From his mid-1950s period, "Blue Haze" (Prestige) is a thoroughly characteristic, moody performance. "Bags' Groove," on which he is joined by Thelonious Monk and vibraphone player

Milt Jackson; "Walkin'" and "Blue 'N Boogie" from an all-star session including J. J. Johnson on trombone, the underappreciated Lucky Thompson on tenor sax, and Horace Silver on piano (Prestige); "Freddie Freeloader" and "All Blues" from the album *Kind of Blue* (Columbia/Legacy); and "Straight No Chaser," "Sid's Ahead," and "Dr. Jackle" from the *Milestones* album (Columbia/Legacy) are all essential. *Miles Smiles* (Columbia/Legacy) contains, besides the blues "Footprints," the extraordinary blues performances "Freedom Jazz Dance" and "Gingerbread Boy."

Charles Mingus loved the blues and played them all the time, even when he wasn't playing them. In addition to the above-mentioned *Blues and Roots*, the individual performances "Folk Forms No. 1" and "MDM" (Candid) are two very different epic blues performances. "Orange Was the Color of Her Dress, Then Blue Silk," from *Mingus at Monterey* (Prestige), is an extended piece with shifting tempos and moods, the high point of which is a long solo, based in the blues but with some alterations, played by altoist Charles McPherson, and is not to be missed. Thelonious Monk also found many ways of dealing with the blues. He recorded his well-known "Blue Monk" many times, notably as a solo on *Thelonious Alone in San Francisco*, and with a quartet on the live album *Thelonious in Action* (both Riverside). "Balue Bolivar Balues-Are," a great performance with Sonny Rollins and bassist Oscar Pettiford, is on *Brilliant Corners* (Riverside), and "Straight No Chaser," from the disc of the same name (Columbia), is probably Monk's most interesting performance of one of his most-often-played compositions.

Tenor saxophonist John Coltrane was a great blues player, and his playing on all material was saturated with blues techniques. In addition to the above-mentioned album *Coltrane Plays the Blues*, a short list of his great blues performances as a leader would have to include "Blue Train" (Blue Note), "Mr. P.C." (Atlantic), "Bessie's Blues," "Chasin' the Trane" (Impulse), and "Sweet Sapphire Blues" (Prestige). "Sweet Sapphire" was originally issued under pianist Red Garland's name; two more powerful Coltrane blues performances still available also under Garland's name are "Soft Winds" and "All Morning Long" (Prestige). Also very much worth hearing are Coltrane's collaboration with vibist Milt Jackson on "The Late, Late Blues" (Atlantic) and his one meeting with his only real tenor peer, Sonny Rollins, on "Tenor Madness" (Prestige). Rollins himself recorded at least one certifiable blues classic, "Blue 7," from the same album, *Saxophone Colossus*, that produced "Moritat" on this book's companion disc. He strikes a similar groove under Miles Davis's leadership on "Vierd Blues," from 1953.

The tenor saxophone has been the vehicle for many definitive blues performances. Gene "Jug" Ammons was one of the earthiest blues players, and his "Hittin' the Jug" (Prestige) has an unforgettable groove. Ammons often teamed up with tenorist Sonny Stitt for an up-tempo blues "tenor battle" they called "Blues Up and Down"; there are good versions on both Prestige and Verve. Dexter Gordon could play some excellent blues, too; two among many good performances are "Stanley the Steamer" and, especially, "The Panther" (Prestige). Zoot Sims recorded one of the first, if not *the* first, improvised blues to make full use of the extended playing time available on the new long-playing records of the early 1950s; "Zoot Swings the Blues" (Prestige), as it was called, was recorded almost accidentally when Sims got carried away during what should have been a normal-length recording and just kept playing. It is a happy, exciting track. Ben Webster was another world-champion blues player; a few standout Webster tracks would have to include "See You at the Fair" (Impulse), "Soulville," "Jive at Six" (Verve), and "Better Go" with trumpeter Harry "Sweets" Edison (Columbia). And Coleman Hawkins did some great extended blues performances during the LP era; among the standouts are "C'mon In" (Prestige); "Bird of Prey Blues" (London); "Algiers Bounce," under the leadership of trumpeter Henry "Red" Allen (RCA/BMG); and his solo on vocalist Abbey Lincoln's recording of Thelonious Monk's "Blue Monk" (Candid).

Drummer Art Blakey was a major proponent of the blues with his band the Jazz Messengers. Probably his most famous recording was the blues "Moanin'" (Blue Note), with its classic solos by trumpeter Lee Morgan and saxophonist Benny Golson. Also not to be missed are the up-tempo blues "Wee Dot" and the medium-tempo "Now's the Time," recorded under Blakey's leadership at Birdland in 1954 with trumpeter Clifford Brown, altoist Lou Donaldson, and pianist Horace Silver (Blue Note). Silver, one of Blakey's original partners in the Jazz Messengers, was a deeply blues-rooted pianist and composer who went on to record many blues and blues-oriented tunes of all types under his own name; the most infectious may well be the happy romp "Filthy McNasty," recorded live at the Village Gate (Blue Note). And organ master Jimmy Smith was nothing if not a blues specialist; two of his best recordings are the 20-minute-long blues extravaganza "The Sermon," with its smoky groove and solos by Lee Morgan, guitarist Kenny Burrell, altoist Lou Donaldson, and little-known tenorist Tina Brooks; and "Midnight Special," with some very late-night tenor saxophone from Stanley Turrentine (both on Blue Note).

Among other remarkable blues performances of the 1950s and 1960s that should be mentioned are three alto saxophone–led tracks: Jackie McLean's "Lights Out" (Prestige), Cannonball

Adderley's "Spontaneous Combustion" (Savoy), and Ornette Coleman's "Ramblin'" (Atlantic). Guitarist Wes Montgomery's extremely relaxed and atmospheric "D-Natural Blues" (Riverside) and his swinging "No Blues," recorded at the Half Note with Wynton Kelly on piano (Verve), are both standout performances. Dizzy Gillespie's big band performed two extroverted blues, "School Days" and "Dizzy's Blues," live at the Newport Jazz Festival (Verve). Trombonist Vic Dickenson was the leader for the medium-up-tempo blues "Sir Charles at Home" (Vanguard), a really inspired gathering of "mainstream" jazz players including the undersung clarinetist Edmond Hall. Multi-reedman Eric Dolphy put some blues in everything he did; one excellent up-tempo track under his leadership is "Bird's Mother," also known as "Mrs. Parker of K.C.," from the disc *Far Cry* (Prestige), on which he plays bass clarinet alongside trumpeter Booker Little, pianist Jaki Byard, Ron Carter on bass, and Roy Haynes on drums.

Finally, one video suggestion. One of the great blues performances of all time was captured by television cameras in 1957 and is available in various forms. The CBS special *The Sound of Jazz* had many highlights, but the highest was the long performance of the blues "Fine and Mellow" sung by Billie Holiday. Her vocal—poignant, salty, plaintive, and defiant all at the same time—alternates with solos by Coleman Hawkins, Gerry Mulligan, Ben Webster, Lester Young, Vic Dickenson, and trumpeter Roy Eldridge, who shakes the roof with his two nasty climactic blues choruses. If you want to see and hear the blues played by great jazz musicians so that you can really feel the meaning of it, you might want to start right here.

Ellington with brass section, 1960. Photograph © Herb Snitzer.

Three

Forms

The blues, as we have seen, can be said to be a form—a short, recurring, cyclical form, over which jazz musicians make a series of variations. A performance could, in principle, go on forever, adding one more "chorus," or round of variations, ad infinitum. This fact, in itself, may be said to be a formal aspect of much jazz—the organization into these cyclical choruses.

Jazz musicians often play in forms more intricate than the blues, and this chapter will look at some of them. Most of them have in common this modular quality, the repetition of a certain set of harmonic and rhythmic facts in the same order, out of which the improviser makes his or her variations. There are other kinds of forms, too—multipart forms, as in ragtime, for example, or open forms in which the duration of various sections is flexible.

And beyond the form of the individual chorus, there is the form of a performance as a whole. The overall form of most jazz performances is determined by the ebb and flow of ideas and dialogue over the course of a series of choruses, with no deliberate planning of the overarching structure—it's like a city that grows up building by building with no advance planning. But in the work of composers such as Duke Ellington, Jelly Roll Morton, and Charles Mingus, there is a development over the entire course of a given piece, not just in each chorus, as you can hear in the companion disc's "U.M.M.G." Although this track consists of a series of choruses, there is a progression in density, volume, and intensity over the course of the performance, which gives it a larger arc of meaning and formal interest. Such performances are more like cities that have been built according to an advance plan. To begin with, though, we will concentrate on the modular element, the form of the chorus itself, and some variations on it.

~~~

After the blues, by far the most common form in classic jazz is the 32-bar American popular song. Of course, there is no single form for the popular song; the classic American popular songs of the 1920s through the 1940s, which formed the basis of so much jazz even into the 1950s and 1960s, do not follow one strict formal pattern; they are marked, at their best, by extraordinary variety. But most of them also have certain resemblances to one another.

The most basic resemblance is this: They are short. If you were to sing a song such as, say, "Pennies from Heaven" one time through, the performance would be over very quickly. Performances of songs such as "Pennies from Heaven"—or "I Got Rhythm," or "Body and Soul," or "How High the Moon," or almost any of the other popular songs that musicians call "standards"—consist, in fact, of repetitions of the song, with variations, just as a blues performance consists of repetitions of the little 12-

bar blues form. But most popular song forms last a bit longer than the blues' brief 12 bars, and they often cover a somewhat broader harmonic territory. Jazz performances of these songs resemble jazz performances of the blues in that they usually consist of a series of improvised variations taken, in turn, by whichever members of the band are designated to take solos.

To envision this chorus structure, it might be helpful to imagine a game, such as Monopoly, in which play consists of circuits around a board. Each trip around the board can be thought of as a chorus; every time the group passes "Go," a new chorus begins. The trip around the perimeter of the board is divided into units of equal dimension, like the properties in Monopoly, or the minute markings on a clock. As they move around the board at a constant rate of speed, which is the song's tempo, jazz musicians are constantly aware of where they are in the form of the chorus. One chorus—one time around the "game board"—of the most common type of popular song lasts 32 bars. After 32 bars, the musicians hit "Go" and begin another cycle. Each bar, it should be added, usually contains four even beats, or quarter notes, at whatever tempo the group has chosen.

It helps that those 32-bar choruses are themselves divided into smaller sections, arranged in very specific ways. The most common of these is referred to as the AABA form. This type of song is divided into four equal groups of 8 bars apiece (like the four sides of a square game board). The first and second 8-bar groups (the first two A's) of each chorus are the same, or very similar. Then there is a third, contrasting 8-bar section, which is the B part. This B part provides contrast and release, and is usually called the "bridge." Then there is a recapitulation of the A section, a kind of final straightaway, after which the form begins again.

"I Got Rhythm," "Body and Soul," "The Way You Look To-night," "Crazy Rhythm," "Blue Moon," "It's Only a Paper Moon," "The Lady Is a Tramp," "S'wonderful," "Old Man River," "Back in Your Own Backyard," and "I Cover the Waterfront" all follow the AABA format. So do Hank Williams's "Hey Good Lookin'," John Lennon and Paul McCartney's "I Feel Fine," and countless others from outside the standard jazz repertoire.

The clearest example of AABA construction on this book's companion disc is "The Eternal Triangle." This performance is, in fact, a kind of extended essay on the AABA form. After a short, punchy intro, the three horns (trumpeter Dizzy Gillespie and tenor saxophonists Sonny Rollins and Sonny Stitt) begin the melody proper with the first A section, at 0:10. At this fast tempo the sections roll around quickly; the A part is repeated at 0:17, then the B part, or the bridge, begins at 0:24. Notice the contrast of this B section, with its longer note values, against the rapid-fire A section; the function of the bridge is to provide this kind of alternative material. When the A part returns, at 0:31, the effect is satisfying.

When Sonny Rollins begins his tenor saxophone solo at 0:39, he is commencing a series of improvised variations on this AABA form, which he will follow for the rest of his solo. You can keep track and practice listening for the chorus form: Rollins begins new choruses at the 1:05, 1:32, 1:58, and 2:25 marks. Listen to several of these, keeping aware of the sections in the AABA form, and you will begin to get a feel for what is going on. At 2:55, Sonny Stitt enters for his own, longer series of choruses (his chorus really begins at 2:52, but Rollins goes over the end of *his* own chorus by just a bit, and Stitt gives him a moment to leave the stage). His new choruses begin at 3:18, 3:44, 4:10, 4:37, 5:03, 5:29, and 5:55.

At 6:21, Rollins returns, and he and Stitt begin a long series of exchanges, as described in chapter 1, and at 8:55 Dizzy Gillespie comes in for his trumpet solo. The important thing to remember, for the purposes of this chapter, is that although this extended (over 14 minutes) performance may seem like a long patrol into uncharted territory, on the most basic level it consists of the same 32-bar form played over and over. Like the blues, this kind of chorus form consists of cycles of beginning, middle, and end, which may be repeated for as long as the musicians like. The musicians are constantly oriented, because they are all moving around the same "game board" at the same rate, so they always know where they are in the form—what "square" they are on, so to speak. It provides a modular structure out of which variations are spun, limited only by the players' imaginations. The interest is generated by the ingenuity of the variations, the quickness of wit, and the musical intelligence displayed. It is analogous in this respect to the theme-and-variations form in European classical music.

The AABA form is hardly the only song form used by jazz musicians. Even within the basic AABA template, there are a number of common variants; sometimes the second A part is slightly altered, as in "Get Happy," or "When You're Smiling," or "Somebody Loves Me." Often the final A section, after the bridge, has a slight extension, called a "tag," as in "I Didn't Know What Time It Was." One of the most popular tunes among jazz musicians, "All the Things You Are," has an ABCA structure—an 8-bar A section, an echoing but reharmonized version of similar melodic material in the 8-bar B section, a contrasting bridge that we can call C, and a reprise of the 8-bar A section, with a four-bar tag appended. Cole

Porter's "Love for Sale" is an interesting variant: The tune is AABA in construction, but it lasts for 64 bars instead of 32—each section is just twice as long.

There are other 32-bar tunes that do not conform to the AABA setup, and they are some of the most popular songs among jazz musicians. "How High the Moon," "All God's Children Got Rhythm," "Indiana," and "Whispering" are all 32 bars, but instead of following the four-part AABA format, or some variant of it, these songs are divided into two 16-bar halves—we could call the halves A1 and A2. Usually these two halves resemble each other, though the second half takes a different turn from the first half. But a performance of one of these tunes still consists of the 32-bar form played over and over, just as with the AABA form; the 32 bars are just divided up differently.

"Moritat"—better known as "Mack the Knife"—as performed by Sonny Rollins on track 4, is one of these 32-bar, two-part, 16-bar-plus-16-bar tunes, but the two halves are basically identical. The melody is familiar, and once around the game board consists of a set of two of these 16-bar units. After playing the theme (into which he interpolates small passing variations, almost as if in dialogue with himself), Rollins begins a series of four improvised choruses, his improvisations lasting until he has said what he had to say. Because each chorus consists of the same 16-bar cycle played twice, it can be hard for a listener to tell when choruses actually begin and end. Here, Rollins's choruses last approximately 46 seconds, so new choruses begin at around 0:46, 1:31, 2:17, and 3:03. Because of the way he plays, you will hear references to the melody popping up from time to time.

All the musicians need to keep in mind where they are in the form of the tune, or they will not be able to come back in together at key points and may not even end together. Notice that this quartet appears to skirt the edges of this situation here. When Rollins is finished, he gives way to pianist Tommy Flanagan for two choruses, and then Rollins comes back in for a series of exchanges with drummer Max Roach, leading into solos by Roach and bassist Doug Watkins. But these exchanges and solos are staggered, divided up trickily, and it is easy to lose track of where you are.

As a listening exercise, try to keep track in this section, beginning at 5:21, with this as a guide: Rollins and drummer Roach play a chorus and a half (32 bars plus 16 bars) of 4-bar exchanges. Roach plays the second half of that second chorus (16 bars) by himself, solo, and then continues for the first half of the next chorus (another 16 bars). Now we are at the midpoint of a chorus, and bassist Watkins enters, playing a solo for the second half of that chorus (16 bars), plus a complete new chorus (32 bars), before Rollins comes back in for the final chorus of the performance. After 16 bars, though, the drums shift back to the style of accompaniment they played over the initial theme statement at the beginning of the track—and the ear is tricked into thinking that this is the beginning of the final chorus. It is in fact the midpoint of the final chorus, as we see after 16 more bars, when Rollins plays a slow phrase, cuing everyone to slow to a stop while he plays his final cadenza.

Confused? They may conceivably have been, too, but Rollins, at least, was apparently keeping track of it all, and the number of choruses totes up evenly by the end. The reason it is tricky is that the ear is trained by experience to hear the entry of a new solo voice as the beginning of a new chorus. But in this section of this performance, the entries are staggered; solos begin at the midpoints of choruses and continue into a next chorus, giving way to another soloist, and so on. Musicians have to concentrate hard in order to always be aware of where they are in the form, especially when they decide to play around with the form.

For another interesting example of musicians using the chorus form in an unusual way, listen to Stan Getz's "I Can't Get Started." Certain choices were clearly made here that lend the track an unusual formal interest, aside from its obvious beauty. For one thing, there is no presentation of the familiar melody of the song. In fact, Getz chooses to begin this AABA-structured song in the middle—at the B part, or bridge—as if taking up a conversation in mid-sentence. Aside from glancing, sidelong references to the melody (as well as to a familiar jazz arrangement of the melody), Getz's solo is a long, extended improvisation on the harmony of the song, abetted by Kenny Barron's extraordinary piano playing. When Getz is finished, Barron takes over for a solo, and here another interesting choice is made—whether in advance or spontaneously on the bandstand, we don't know. The performance ends on Barron's piano, without Getz returning, a very unusual strategy, and so effective here.

<center>~~~~</center>

But most performances of blues or other chorus-based jazz standards follow the format of a procession of conventionally structured choruses. A performance like "Moritat," or "The Eternal Triangle," could, in principle, go on forever; there is no inherent aesthetic reason for the performance to stop at any point, assuming that the musicians could keep inventing interesting variations. The reason why such performances end are largely mechanical. When musicians were playing for dancers, the individual songs' lengths were limited by the needs of the dancers for relief and variety. In the days of 78-rpm records—in jazz's earliest years up until the very early 1950s—performance length on records was dictated by the fact that only about three minutes of music could fit on one side of a disc, as you can hear on the companion CD's "Weather Bird Rag" and "Boogie Woogie," both recorded on 78s. This limitation changed when long-playing records arrived in the 1950s, and continuous performances the length of "The Eternal Triangle" and "Moritat" could be recorded. But even these were limited by the amount of time available on an LP record.

Beyond that, performances are limited by the audience's—or the musicians'!—attention span. Even the most inventive players run out of things to say on a given tune on a given evening. But this is different than saying that there is an inherent aesthetic, formal reason for bringing a performance to a close. Running out of things to say is not the same as summing things up. Performances such as "Boogie Woogie," "Moritat," and "The Eternal Triangle" are mainly *about* the series of choruses, the variations. There isn't really a larger arc to the performance, except what the musicians can generate together, as they go. A bare-bones sense of beginning and ending is provided by the statement of the theme at the beginning and end of the performance, but the journey itself depends on the improvisations.

"U.M.M.G.," as played by the Duke Ellington Orchestra with trumpeter Dizzy Gillespie as guest soloist, is something else again. As you will hear, this performance also consists of a series of choruses, but here, the entire performance has an arc, carefully arranged by a central, organizing intelligence—in this case a collaboration between Duke Ellington and his musical alter ego, Billy Strayhorn. The track begins softly and builds to a crescendo over the course of its first four minutes, with more and more instruments being added to the mix as it goes along. This progression was not the result of improvisation; it was deliberately orchestrated to create an intended picture. Yet considerable room is left for solo voices to improvise, and the track is, in effect, a concerto for trumpet and orchestra.

The role of the composer in jazz has always raised a question, among critics at least. If the essence of jazz is improvisation, the question runs, is the term "jazz composer" an oxymoron? The beginnings of an answer may be found in the fact that jazz always represents a tension between planned elements and improvised elements. From almost the beginnings of jazz, some figures have been interested in making structured settings in which the characteristic elements of jazz—among them the peculiar relations between foreground and background, blues tonality, and certain characteristic rhythmic elements—could be found, but arranged deliberately by a composer's organizing intelligence. The New Orleans pianist and composer Jelly Roll Morton is generally recognized as having been the first real jazz composer in this sense.

The larger the ensemble, of course, the clearer is the need for someone to take charge and give a structure to the proceedings. As big bands became popular through the 1920s, there arose a class of composer and orchestrator (also commonly known as an "arranger") who could shape a structure for a performance in which individual improvisations would be set off by contrasting material written out for the ensemble. Among all these composer-arrangers, the one who had the greatest imagination, the broadest reach, and the most profound musical influence was Duke Ellington. Some listeners will always prefer to hear a group of musicians get together and jam, but those who also enjoy hearing a compositional intelligence at work recognize Duke Ellington as the master.

"U.M.M.G." is a fine example not just of the way the Ellington orchestra mediated between solo voices and the ensemble, as discussed in chapter 1, but of the way Ellington and Strayhorn could construct a performance that had a compositional, formal point transcending the work of the soloists. It progresses from Gillespie's muted opening musings, accompanied only by bass and drums, through a gradually escalating series of variations on the tune's theme, handed off between soloist and ensemble, to a terrific climax played by the entire band in full roar; the music then tapers off, cools down, to a point where Gillespie is again playing muted, first over only bass accompaniment, and finally, unaccompanied; when Gillespie brings this coda to a close, the entire band shouts out one final exclamation point.

Ellington and Strayhorn organized this performance around a series of choruses, just as the other tracks we have looked at so far have been based around a series of choruses. The choruses of "U.M.M.G." conform, in fact, to a classic 32-bar AABA structure, which we can see most clearly here in the first full ensemble chorus, beginning at 1:33—an 8-bar A section (stated by the saxophones), then a repetition of that A section, with slight variations (beginning at 1:44), then a contrasting 8-bar B section (beginning at 1:54), and a return to a slightly altered A section, beginning at 2:04 (slightly difficult to recognize here because clarinetist Jimmy Hamilton continues playing after the B section). At 2:14 a new chorus begins with the reentry of Gillespie. This chorus form is repeated for almost the entire length of this performance.

But instead of the choruses functioning only as a series of self-contained units of beginning, middle, and end—and as cues for the entries of new soloists—the cyclical form is used here to progressively up the ante of compositional density, volume, and timbre. Notice that almost every time a new chorus begins, some new element is added to the mix. There is the entry of the saxophones at 1:33, after Gillespie's two opening solo choruses, described in the previous paragraph. When Gillespie's horn brings in the next new chorus at 2:14, he is playing open instead of muted horn, and he is accompanied by a saxophone choir that provides commentary on his improvisations for the length of the chorus. When the next chorus begins, at 2:55, Gillespie again steps out of the way and the trombones charge in, not muted as they were behind the saxophone melody at 1:33, but open and loud, with trumpet and clarinet commentary dancing around them. The chorus form is used here as a compositional principle that builds the performance incrementally to a climax. In this performance, everything has been carefully paced to provide not just a series of varied and interesting choruses, but an overall shape, while still allowing considerable room for individual improvisation.

〰〰

The string-of-choruses form, although it dominated jazz from the late 1920s up through the 1960s, is not the only way to approach jazz. In fact, it is a bit of a puzzle why other forms have not been explored more energetically. Of these other possible forms, the most significant is probably the segmented, multistrain approach characteristic of ragtime music and very common in the early jazz recordings that came out of New Orleans.

Ragtime was a precursor to jazz. It was a syncopated music that drew on African American rhythmic and expressive elements. The most famous ragtime composer was undoubtedly

Scott Joplin, the composer of "Maple Leaf Rag," "The Entertainer," and dozens of other ragtime classics. The early ragtime composers, such as Joplin, James Scott, and Joseph Lamb, thought of themselves—not inaccurately—as serious composers contributing something new and significant to the stream of classical piano music, although as ragtime became a popular phenomenon, even a craze, in the early years of the twentieth century, popular songwriters such as Irving Berlin began to write catchy pop tunes using ragtime techniques.

It is hard to overstate the influence that ragtime had at that time on popular music, especially on the fledgling jazz bands of New Orleans. Although Joplin, like his nearest peer, James Scott, was from Missouri, and ragtime was in fact largely a midwestern phenomenon, this music likely made its way to New Orleans via the tour boats of the Mississippi River, and it there found fertile soil in which to grow and mutate. Many of the early New Orleans jazz bands, in fact, called themselves "ragtime orchestras" and drew repertoire from the music of Joplin and other ragtime composers, and also came up with their own ragtime-based jazz originals such as the famous "Tiger Rag."

Ragtime compositions, instead of consisting of a modular arrangement of the same chorus over and over, are segmented; they contain three or four different sections of contrasting thematic material, called strains, each a self-contained unit, arranged for maximum contrast. Seen against the relatively simple AABA popular-song structure we have been looking at, a typical ragtime piece, like the familiar "Maple Leaf Rag," may have a form with strains arranged in a pattern like this: AABBACCDD. Each of those strains lasts considerably longer than the 8-bar sections of the AABA songs.

A classic example is King Oliver's 1923 recording of "Weather Bird Rag"—in some ways the most formally complex of all the performances on the accompanying disc. "Weather Bird Rag" was composed, in fact, by Louis Armstrong, who plays cornet in this performance next to his mentor, King Oliver. The piece's structure is worth going into in some detail, because the variety and amount of ground covered in such a brief (under three minutes) recording is really remarkable. The performance begins with a brief (4 bars) introduction by the band; at 0:04 the first (A) strain (16 bars) begins, and at 0:22 it repeats. At 0:41 a second (B) strain (also 16 bars) is introduced, played through, and repeated at 0:59. After this repeat, the first (A) theme is restated, beginning at 1:18. When this is finished, there is a very brief (4 bars) fanfarelike transitional moment at 1:36, and then at 1:41 a third (C) strain (also 16 bars) begins with a trombone break. At 1:59 this section repeats, beginning with a banjo break, and then at 2:18 it begins yet a third time, this time with a clarinet break. At 2:36, with the third section finished, the horns play a little tag and everything closes out.

This very tight form is designed, in effect, to say something about the ensemble, about the music itself, rather than about the individual soloist. A fascinating comparison may be made between the Oliver recording of "Weather Bird Rag" and Armstrong's revisitation of the same tune five years later, after he was well established as a solo performer and a star in his own right. Now titled simply "Weather Bird," it is a wild and stunningly inventive duet with the great pianist Earl Hines. If you know the Oliver recording, the Armstrong/Hines version will be even more amazing to you than it might be otherwise; it follows exactly the same scheme as the Oliver version, except that the first A section is played through only once (once through A, twice through B, then once through A again), and the C section is played through only twice. This shortening, which resembles how a classical musician might leave out repeats at his or her discretion, is done to make room for an extended coda where Hines and Armstrong play exchanges over a dominant and diminished chord before bringing it in for a landing. Although billed as a trumpet solo with piano accompaniment, it is anything but; the two voices are nearly equal, the performance is about their interaction. It is worth making the effort to find.

Further Listening:

Forms

To experience the modular, chorus-based form of a jazz performance, you almost need do no more than close your eyes and
point to the jazz section at a record store. The great majority of jazz
recordings are based on the kinds of modular song forms discussed in this chapter. Many of the most famous and well-loved
recordings follow this form and give maximum space for the improvised variations of the great jazz soloists. Lionel Hampton's
small-band sessions of the 1930s (RCA/BMG); Teddy Wilson's
great 1930s sessions with Billie Holiday (Columbia/Legacy);
Benny Goodman's trio and quartet sessions with Lionel Hampton,
Teddy Wilson, and Gene Krupa (RCA/BMG), and his sextet recordings with guitar genius Charlie Christian (Columbia/Legacy);
Gypsy guitarist Django Reinhardt's recordings with the Quintet of
the Hot Club of France (available on countless labels, both domes-
tic and import); the 1938 Kansas City Six recordings with Lester
Young and Buck Clayton (Commodore); guitarist and bandleader
Eddie Condon's many Chicago-style jam session recordings (Com-
modore and Columbia/Legacy); Coleman Hawkins's classic 1939
performance of "Body and Soul" (RCA/BMG); the majority of
Charlie Parker's small-group recordings (Savoy, Dial, Verve); Miles
Davis's quintet recordings with John Coltrane (Prestige, Colum-
bia/Legacy); Davis's classic album *Kind of Blue* (Columbia/Legacy);
John Coltrane's "Giant Steps" (Atlantic); and countless more cen-

ter around the ability of musicians to play a series of improvised variations on a short cyclical form.

That being said, jazz music has also been the occasion for a lot of musical thinking that has gone beyond an overwhelming focus on the series of improvised choruses, and has involved more of a compositional intelligence. Naturally, big bands have made extensive use of orchestrators and arrangers who would shape performances (many of which consisted, when you get right down to it, of a series of choruses) and orchestrate them for four or five trumpets, several trombones, five saxophones, and rhythm. The line between the arranger, who is primarily an interpreter and an orchestrator of songs written by others, and a genuine composer, who comes up with original thematic material, original orchestration, and original structural elements, is sometimes a fine one in jazz, which is after all a music where every individual who solos on a composition generates original thematic material.

Fletcher Henderson was jazz's first composer/arranger, and he created the template on which most of the subsequent big-band arranging of the 1920s and 1930s depended. His recorded work is discussed in "Further Listening" for chapter 1, and his recordings often contain elements that are interesting formally, as do those of his contemporaries Don Redman, Horace Henderson, and Benny Carter. The three-disc set *A Study in Frustration* (Columbia/Legacy) is the place to go to understand the development of the work of this extremely important figure. Likewise, the sometimes elaborately orchestrated work that arranger Bill Challis did for Paul Whiteman's orchestra in the late 1920s (RCA/BMG) contained all sorts of ambitious and unusual formal elements.

In the 1930s and 1940s, with the proliferation of big bands, many fine composer/arrangers came to prominence, among them

Mary Lou Williams (who played and arranged for Andy Kirk's band, as well as contributing arrangements to the bands of Benny Goodman and others), Eddie Sauter, Ralph Burns, Tadd Dameron, Gerry Mulligan, and Gil Evans. One of the most interesting figures from a compositional standpoint was George Russell; his pairing of "Cubana Be" and "Cubana Bop," recorded by Dizzy Gillespie's big band in 1947 (RCA/BMG), was an ambitious melding of Afro-Cuban musical elements with jazz big-band orchestration. Other recordings by Russell are also mentioned in chapter 1.

Most of these master orchestrators composed their own material as well as orchestrating others' work for large ensembles. But there have been certain figures in jazz whose primary ambition has plainly been to generate original thematic, conceptual, and orchestrational totalities—complete compositions, to project a complete vision of music. Among these, the three towering figures have undoubtedly been Jelly Roll Morton, Duke Ellington, and Charles Mingus.

New Orleans pianist Ferdinand "Jelly Roll" Morton is generally regarded as the first true jazz composer. Before him had come the ragtime composers, Scott Joplin and company, as well as popular-tune writers whose products jazz musicians had turned to their own uses. But Morton was apparently the first to write through-composed pieces for jazz band that used not just ragtime-based syncopations but all the compositional elements central to jazz— the riffs, breaks, blues tonality, call-and-response techniques—to create total compositions. In his recordings with the band he called his Red Hot Peppers, Morton, beginning in 1926 (RCA/ BMG), created a body of compositions thoroughly integrated with their orchestration for the classic New Orleans ensemble of trumpet (or cornet), trombone, clarinet, piano, banjo, bass, and drums.

His most characteristic compositions were often segmented, like ragtime, with different strains, and they often seemed to be *about* themselves in a way that clearly indicated that Morton knew he was doing something significant, and that seemed, also, to be about the nature of jazz itself. A perfect example that can stand for many is the very first recording he made with the Red Hot Peppers, the 1926 "Black Bottom Stomp." The piece is in two parts, each of which has a distinct flavor and is organized around a motif. The first section seems to hark back to a slightly stiffer, earlier form of orchestrated ragtime, almost like marching-band music; after a dramatic fanfare, the piece shifts gears into a more headlong, forward-moving section, as if to say, "That was then, this is now," with the instruments arranged in a relationship more closely resembling the classic New Orleans ensemble format, and organized around a little repeated "Hold that tiger" rhythmic motif. There are breaks, riffs, and solo passages for clarinet, piano, cornet, and banjo. Listen closely, also, to the bass on this track; it shifts back and forth between playing on every other beat, as a tuba might, and on every beat (this is especially easy to hear during the banjo solo). The detailing and variety presented in this track, which lasts barely over three minutes, is astonishing. But so is almost all of the music that Morton recorded with this ensemble of shifting personnel.

Duke Ellington picked up, in a sense, where Morton left off. His significant recordings began in the late mid-1920s, right around the same time as Morton's, and he also loved to use New Orleans musicians. But his imagination ranged more widely than Morton's, and he developed an orchestra to play his compositions, which he led continuously for fifty years. Ultimately, he was to become the most important and influential composer in the jazz idiom; the subtlety, variety, and profundity of Ellington's imagination outstripped that of everyone else. Even on material based on a series-of-choruses form (such as "U.M.M.G."), Ellington displayed an amazing creative imagination for overall structure, pacing, and drama.

A phenomenal example—one of the most phenomenal in the history of recorded jazz—is "Diminuendo and Crescendo in Blue," recorded live at the Newport Jazz Festival in 1956 (Columbia/Legacy). Although originally recorded in 1937 as two sides of a 78-rpm record, this extended performance from 1956 has assumed a deserved legendary status. The composition, basically a series of blues choruses, is divided into two halves. The first half begins loudly, in full orchestrational roar, and gets gradually quieter and simpler; the second half begins more or less quietly and builds to an apocalyptic finale. In the 1950s, Ellington got the idea to insert a tenor saxophone solo, delegated to Paul Gonsalves, between the two halves (Gonsalves's solo is described in chapter 2), but the overall form of the performance, with its attention to dynamics, texture, and dramatic development, is one of the great edifices of jazz music.

But Ellington also concerned himself with forms that were not based solely on the procession-of-choruses model. Two of his best-known early compositions, "Black and Tan Fantasy" and "East St. Louis Toodle-Oo," are segmented, almost like ragtime pieces, with different strains, though with an additional variety and depth stemming from Ellington's deliberate use not just of certain instruments for certain parts but certain specific players on those instruments. Later extended pieces such as "Black, Brown, and Beige" (in a stunning version, with vocals by Mahalia Jackson, on Columbia/Legacy), "A Tone Parallel to Harlem," and "The Tattooed

Bride" show Ellington engaging the question of how to create a long form that will still have the flexibility and vibrancy of jazz. The Columbia/Legacy albums *Masterpieces by Ellington* (which contains "The Tattooed Bride" as well as extended arrangements of the Ellington songs "Mood Indigo," "Sophisticated Lady," and "Solitude") and *Ellington Uptown* (which contains "A Tone Parallel to Harlem" as well as extended versions of "Take the 'A' Train" and "The Mooch") are real tours de force.

Ellington and his musical partner Billy Strayhorn loved the suite form, the way of gathering together disparate pieces in different dance rhythms that stretches back to the baroque. The disc *Three Suites* (Columbia/Legacy) contains their reworking of Tchaikovsky's *Nutcracker Suite* and Grieg's *Peer Gynt;* other landmarks using this technique include the *Far East Suite* (RCA/BMG), *Such Sweet Thunder* (Columbia/Legacy), *Latin American Suite* (Fantasy), and *The Ellington Suites* (Pablo), which includes "The Queen's Suite," one of the finest things Ellington wrote. Greatest of all, perhaps, is the score for the 1959 movie *Anatomy of a Murder* (Columbia/Legacy), in which a double set of themes is maintained, reorchestrated, and relit over the symphony-length performance with extraordinary resourcefulness and shattering emotional impact.

Bassist and composer Charles Mingus, whose heroes were Duke Ellington and Charlie Parker, used the harmonic vocabulary of bop and the compositional and structural ambitions of Ellington to create a body of fascinating and complex work. One classic example is "Orange Was the Color of Her Dress, Then Blue Silk," recorded at the Monterey Jazz Festival (Prestige). The piece shifts terrain and tempo constantly, with room open, in true Ellingtonian fashion, for solo statements, the most remarkable of which, here, is the long solo by alto saxophonist Charles McPherson, during which a unique and uncanny mood settles. The album *Mingus Presents Mingus* (Candid) contains four pieces—"Fables of Faubus," "Folk Forms No. 1," "All the Things You Could Be by Now if Sigmund Freud's Wife Was Your Mother," and "What Love"—each of which presents a different set of formal elements and is full of roiling stop-time passages, tempo shifts, group improvisation, arranged backgrounds to solos, dynamic contrast, and volatile moods. On *Blues and Roots* (Atlantic), the track "My Jelly Roll Soul" is a canny homage to Jelly Roll Morton; like Morton's "Black Bottom Stomp," it alternates between a 2-beat feel and a straight-ahead 4/4. Mingus's recordings are wildly uneven, but few are uninteresting from a formal perspective. Other Mingus recordings to check out are mentioned in "Further Listening" in chapter 1.

Not all small-group recordings are without formal interest beyond the string-of-choruses format, of course. Louis Armstrong's 1928 "Beau Koo Jack" (Columbia/Legacy), by a somewhat expanded version of his Hot Seven configuration, is a very ambitiously routined performance. Likewise the late-1920s recordings led by saxophonist Frank Trumbauer (Columbia/Legacy), with bands of shifting personnel, consisting mostly of musicians associated with the Paul Whiteman and Jean Goldkette orchestras, especially cornet legend Bix Beiderbecke. The Trumbauer recordings often have very intricate compositional aspects and unusual formal preoccupations. The 1930s recordings of the small band led by bassist John Kirby (Columbia/Legacy) were carefully arranged miniatures, full of detail and interesting routining, as were many of the small-band recordings led by members of Duke Ellington's orchestra (RCA/BMG). For a special treat, track down a 1945

Ellington-led trio performance of the old folk standard "Frankie and Johnny" (RCA/BMG), a fascinating multipart conversation among Ellington's piano, Junior Raglin's bass, and Sonny Greer's drums.

Many of the early bebop recordings showed a much greater concern for routining than later bop records, and they incorporated interesting compositional elements, especially the early Dizzy Gillespie/Charlie Parker recordings, such as "Dizzy Atmosphere," "Groovin' High," and even "Salt Peanuts," with its interesting transitions and breaks (Guild/Musicraft). Charlie Parker's 1947 Dial recording of his own unusually structured composition "Klactoveedsedstene" is an example of the great alto saxophone genius thinking in real compositional terms. Pianist Bud Powell's 1951 masterpiece "Un Poco Loco" (Blue Note) contains extended improvisation, after the initial theme, over an open form based on a drone, without a chorus structure, over which Powell plays until he has had his say. Powell's 1953 trio recording of "Glass Enclosure" (Blue Note) is a tightly controlled composition with several strains, shifting tempos, and arranged elements for bass and drums, all in two and a half minutes.

Likewise, Thelonious Monk's series of late-1940s and early-1950s recordings for Blue Note are full of interesting compositional material. Monk's later recordings often contain unusual structural or formal aspects. His composition "Brilliant Corners," from the Riverside album of the same title, is a mysterious theme in an AABA form, played slowly and menacingly at first, then played through, again, at double tempo. When the soloists play their solos, they too play over this background of alternating tempos. One lesser-known Monk tune worth looking at is "Light Blue" (available on Riverside's live 1958 set *Thelonious in Action*), which consists of the same 8-bar theme played twice, over completely different harmony.

～～～

As mentioned, the advent of the long-playing record in the early 1950s allowed musicians greater space in which to explore the possibilities not just of extended soloing but of recording compositions with extended forms, transitions into various sections, and the like. Duke Ellington and Charles Mingus made full use of this new freedom, but they were far from the only ones to do so.

One of the most notable fruits of this increased space and time was a crop of recordings by composer/instrumentalists who were interested in combining elements of jazz and European classical music in wide-ranging compositions that used jazz instrumentation and expanded forms. A great single-disc survey of this movement, called "third-stream" music at the time, is *The Birth of the Third Stream* (Columbia/Legacy); it contains performances of music composed by pianist John Lewis (leader of the Modern Jazz Quartet), classical/jazz genre-breaking composer and critic Gunther Schuller (his *Symphony for Brass and Percussion* is conducted here by the great Dimitri Mitropoulos), George Russell, Jimmy Giuffre, Charles Mingus, and J. J. Johnson. There are featured solos by Miles Davis, pianist Bill Evans, and several other notables. Some of these pieces work better than others, some are exciting indeed and some are on the ponderous side, but everything here is at least thought-provoking to listen to.

Pianist and composer Dave Brubeck, certainly one of the most popular jazz musicians who ever lived, was also always intrigued by possible links between European classical forms and techniques and jazz. In particular, he loved playing in uncommon meters, and his famous quartet with alto saxophonist Paul Desmond was, among other things, a workshop for different approaches to rhythm and form. His albums, especially *Time Out* (Columbia/Legacy), which contains the very famous tune "Take Five," in the rarely used 5/4 meter, reached a large and enthusiastic audience.

Sonny Rollins's 1958 "Freedom Suite," from the album of the same name (Riverside), is an intriguingly structured original composition by Rollins for a trio including Rollins, bassist Oscar Pettiford, and drummer Max Roach. Weighing in at nearly twenty minutes, the piece cleaves into four major sections, often incorporating improvisation over a shifting set of givens, including different tempos and time signatures. It is one of the most interesting extended frameworks ever devised for a small jazz group. The same may be said of *A Love Supreme*, recorded in 1964 by the John Coltrane Quartet (Impulse). A suite in four parts with a specifically spiritual dimension, *A Love Supreme* took up the entire LP on which it was originally issued. Each of the four sections has its own tempo and mood, and yet they coalesce, ultimately, into an overwhelming and unified statement. It is one of the most powerful things the tenor saxophone giant ever recorded, and also one of the most formally ambitious.

Miles Davis's quintet of the mid-1960s, heard on the companion disc's "Footprints," with tenor saxophonist Wayne Shorter, pianist Herbie Hancock, bassist Ron Carter, and drummer Tony Williams, was definitely one of the most adventuresome groups of that time. On discs like *Miles Smiles, Sorcerer, Nefertiti, Water Babies, Filles de Kilimanjaro*, and *ESP* (Columbia/Legacy), as well as slightly later efforts with slightly different personnel, such as *In a Silent Way, A Tribute to Jack Johnson*, and *Bitches Brew* (Columbia/

Legacy), Davis and company explored all kinds of ways of stretching and bending form, occasionally using open-ended sections for improvisation, in which a change to a new section would be signaled by the soloist, rather than conforming to a prearranged form. They used other ingenious and unusual approaches, such as that on the title track of *Nefertiti*, where the trumpet and saxophone play the theme over and over while the rhythm instruments improvise around the recurring melody; the track gets louder, softer, denser, and sparer, as if all the members of the band are part of the same living organism—which, in a sense, they are.

Alto saxophonist and composer Ornette Coleman made a name for himself in part by coming up with all kinds of small-group (and, eventually, large-ensemble) settings for group improvisation. Extraordinary compositions such as "Lonely Woman," "Congeniality," "Free," "Forerunner"; the other quartet pieces on albums such as *The Shape of Jazz to Come*, *Change of the Century*, and *This Is Our Music* (Atlantic); the trio performances on *Town Hall, 1962* (ESP), *At the Golden Circle*, volumes 1 and 2, and *The Empty Foxhole* (Blue Note); and so many other compositions he recorded in the 1960s and afterward challenged the common formal assumptions in the jazz of that time by creating melodies of unusual length and open frameworks for improvisation in which the direction of the tune would be led by the players' melodic invention rather than by a predetermined chorus structure. (The Modern Jazz Quartet, by the way, made a fascinating interpretation of "Lonely Woman" on their 1962 Atlantic album of the same name.)

Coleman's 1960 recording *Free Jazz* (Atlantic), recorded by a "double quartet" of two trumpets, two reed players (Coleman on alto and Eric Dolphy on bass clarinet), two bassists, and two drummers, raised rich formal possibilities. By having, in effect, two groups playing simultaneously in two different tempos, Coleman immediately undercut the temporal basis by which form is usually measured in the first place. Yet all the members of the double quartet periodically come together for ensemble passages, different each time, which introduce new sections for improvisation. In other words, the piece, in addition to its other formal interest, references the kind of segmented form associated with ragtime. Even though it is in some ways very challenging listening, *Free Jazz* is, above all, a blast to experience.

Sonny Rollins, 1960. Photograph by Lee Tanner/The Jazz Image.

Four

Improvisation

In the previous chapter we looked at some of the types of formal elements that structure jazz performance. But within any given form, what determines the specific kinds of things a jazz musician will choose to play at any given moment? How can several musicians play together without written music, all of them making spontaneous variations, and not have chaos? What are jazz musicians doing when they improvise?

There are many misconceptions among nonmusicians about the meaning of improvisation. The Latin root literally means unforeseen (*im* + *pro* + *visus*); the Oxford dictionary says that it means to "compose without preparation." But it means this in a very specialized sense. An experienced cook may spontaneously compose a meal at a friend's house, based on the ingredients that happen to be on hand, but years of experience with food and spices will inform the spontaneous choices the cook makes.

So improvisation does not mean leaving things to

chance, at least not in the way that some people might mean it. In jazz, it means to make intelligent choices spontaneously, based on knowledge and experience. There is enormous preparation involved, but it entails acquiring the kinds of proficiencies that allow one to respond quickly to a shifting situation. This chapter will look at some of the kinds of knowledge that allow jazz musicians to make intelligent spontaneous choices.

It should be said at the outset that music made by human beings is never either purely spontaneous or purely planned. Music always exists somewhere on the spectrum between the hypothetical extremes of pure spontaneity and absolute fidelity to a composer's intentions. Some musical situations are closer to the "wholly planned" end of the spectrum, some to the "purely spontaneous." But even the most wholly planned music—a symphony, for example—will always have some variations in performance. One can listen to two versions of Beethoven's Sixth Symphony, one conducted by Herbert von Karajan and one conducted by Fritz Reiner, and they will sound almost like two different pieces of music. There are always questions of interpretation in the human performance of music, and sometimes those questions are settled at the time of performance.

On the other hand, what would "purely spontaneous" music be? Gather five or six people who have never touched an instrument, hand out instruments at random, then give them a signal at which they are all to begin playing. Obviously, the sounds that emerge would be disorganized and meaningless, to say the least. Even the most spontaneous music involves some choices, made beforehand, about tempo, key, and structure.

Improvisation is a prized skill in almost all musical cultures. Johann Sebastian Bach was a legendary improviser on the organ, as were both Mozart and Beethoven on the piano. Indian classical musicians make extended improvisations based on intricate scale patterns and rhythmic patterns, African drummers, Cuban string bands, Bulgarian *gadulka* virtuosos . . . The ability to think on one's feet is a gauge of real knowledge, across cultures and across eras.

Yet the question still arises: Out of what materials are these improvisations spun? Obviously, musicians don't sit down with an empty slate and whip things up out of nothing. All art is composed of variations based partly on memory and partly on imagination. A jazz musician who begins to make improvised variations on "I Got Rhythm" is guided not only by the form of the song but also by all the other performances he or she has heard of "I Got Rhythm," just as anyone improvising anything—cooking a meal, strategizing a football game, carrying on a courtship—will rely on ways in which certain problems have been solved or negotiated in the past.

Still, what is the actual stuff from which the musician spins these variations? The improviser has three basic categories of material with which to create variations; in practice, the three overlap and are interdependent. One is the harmonic structure, the underlying tonal skeleton, of the tune. Another involves rhythm, tempo, and accenting. The third is melodic imagination, harder to define and involving both harmonic and rhythmic factors.

〰〰〰

We looked in the last chapter at the cyclical, or modular, nature of the majority of jazz performances, which consist of the same cyclical form (a chorus) repeated over and over for the length of the performance. Each chorus of a given tune has the same structure and contains its own beginning, middle, and end. The chorus structure gives the improvising musician a template that is analogous to the elements of a story—and not only to beginning, middle, and end, but to tension, momentary resolution, unfulfilled yearning, repetition, change of scene, and so on. Each time through the chorus is a trip through the same small story form, or landscape, like one trip around a Monopoly board. But within these forms, how does the musician know what to play in order to have it make sense with what the other musicians play?

The first answer has to do with the tune's harmonic structure, or blueprint. Every song mentioned in the previous chapter has a harmonic structure that is peculiar to that song and that is related to, but independent of, the song's "official" melody.

Here is a way to visualize this: Think of track 2 on the accompanying disc, "Boogie Woogie." If you could somehow remove the vocal, trumpet, and saxophone parts from the track, leaving only the piano, bass, and drum accompaniment, a musician listening to it would still know that the band was playing the blues.

Or take Sonny Rollins's version of "Moritat," also known as "Mack the Knife." Listen closely in the first chorus, not just to Rollins's melody statement, but to what pianist Tommy Flanagan is playing behind Rollins's melody statement. Underneath, Flanagan is playing a series of chords in a certain order, a harmonic progression on top of which the melody rides comfortably. Most listeners would identify the song by its melody, but here's the thing to know: If Rollins's lead voice were removed somehow, and only the piano, bass, and drums were audible, an experienced musician would still be able to identify the piece as "Mack the Knife."

Virtually every popular song—"I Got Rhythm," "How High the

Moon," "Jingle Bells," "Yesterday," "Summertime"—has something like this: a harmonic structure that is peculiar to that song, and which is recognizable, to musicians, even without the melody. If Sonny Rollins had started to play "Moritat" and Flanagan had begun to play the harmonic structure of "I Got Rhythm," there would have been deep trouble on the bandstand.

So it isn't only the melody that determines the song. There is a kind of understructure that is also peculiar to that song. This harmonic structure bears the same relation to the melody that a story line bears to the actual telling of a story. *Romeo and Juliet* and *West Side Story* have essentially the same story line; the setting is different, the characters have different personalities, but the problems presented in the plot are almost exactly the same—the story of the star-crossed lovers. You could say the same for the relation between *The Odyssey,* James Joyce's *Ulysses,* and the film *O Brother, Where Art Thou?* There is something underneath the actual specifics of a given retelling of a story that is recognizable as the story line. Likewise, there is something underneath the melody of a song that is recognizable as that song's characteristic harmonic progression or structure. But what is that "something"?

To begin to answer this, let's go back to the image of the chorus as a game board. Once a tune is started at a certain tempo, all the musicians in the group move around the game board of the chorus at the same rate. If we visualize a single bar of music as a square of the game board, all the musicians are on the same square at any given moment.

The hypothetical isolated piano part we discussed above consists, mainly, of a series of chords—multiple notes struck at the same time. When the musicians reach a given stretch of the board, the pianist has to play a certain chord for a certain number of "squares" until the time comes to switch to another chord. Within that certain number of squares, the pianist can play that chord whenever and however she or he wants to. A song begins on a certain chord, which controls the harmony for a certain number of bars, or squares, and we know that when we get to, say, the fourth square, the chord will change and the new chord will be in effect for another four, or eight, or two and a half, squares, at which point it will change again, and so on.

Musicians call this progression the "chord changes," or "changes," for short. It is a mutually understood harmonic story line on top of which each musician constructs his own specific retelling of the story. On top of that understructure, one could write an almost infinite number of melodies. The requirement is that they somehow "fit" the understructure, or harmonic "story line." But why do some melodies fit the understructure while others don't?

～～～

On the way to an answer, it might be worth remembering Plato's idea of the existence of "forms"—essentially abstractions that lend conceptual coherence to observable phenomena. The ideal form of "chair," for example, has no actual existence (although Plato thought it did); it is abstract, and visible only in specific examples of "chair," which have infinite variations. Likewise, the harmonic structure of a tune in its pure form exists only in the abstract; it becomes "visible," or hearable, only in the way a given musician gives voice to it. But any given chord can be "voiced" in nearly infinite ways.

For a quick example, if you can get to, or visualize, a piano key-board, play or imagine a C-major chord, consisting simply of the notes C, E, and G. A pianist can "voice" this chord in many ways, which is to say he can deploy these notes in many different configurations around the keyboard. He can choose to invert the second and third notes and play C–G–E. Or, since the same twelve notes repeat themselves in the same order in successive octaves going up the keyboard, he can spread the notes of a chord out, double some of them up. He can play C–G–C–E–G. He can play a C way down in the left hand, with an E an octave and a half above played with the thumb of his left hand (if his hands are big enough), then, with the right hand, play G–C–E. Or he can play any one of countless other permutations. Each one of these voicings can be understood as a C-major chord.

Any chord you can imagine is subject to the same kind of variety of voicings. As pianists accompany a soloist, they are constantly shifting the voicing of these chords to keep things interesting and also to respond to what the soloist plays. There is infinite variety available to the imaginative accompanist, therefore, as well as to the soloist. Listen carefully, for example, to pianist Kenny Barron playing alongside Stan Getz's tenor saxophone on "I Can't Get Started" to see just how supple and imaginative an accompaniment can be. In fact, Barron's playing transcends the concept of accompaniment; it is a full-scale dialogue with the lead voice; Barron combines chords with melodic elements, and echoes the saxophone's phrases, ripostes, small challenges. Yet both players are following the same underlying story line, making variations based on the same chord progression.

The chords that make up that chord progression are not static; they are dynamic. Different types of chords have different effects; they interact with one another to create tension. Then they resolve it. Or they ratchet it up. They may imply a stasis for a moment or two, but underneath they may be posing a lingering question that the next chord casts in a different light. The underlying harmony pulls the ear along a path that unfolds; pressure builds up, steam is let off, enticements are offered, expectations are set up, then fulfilled or subverted, just as in a story told in words. It is up to the improvising musician to elaborate, flesh out, "retell" the story line of any given song in as interesting and individual a way as possible.

If an improvising musician could pick his or her notes only from the three or four tones found in the actual chord of a given passage, his choices would be very limited. So a further, and central, point for the improvising musician is that each chord that makes up the chord progression of a tune has associated with it a scale—a series of other notes, in addition to those in the chord proper, that are implied by the chord. In our C-major chord, for example, the obvious scale would be a C-major scale. If you start on the note C and sing "do-re-mi-fa-so-la-ti-do," you will sing a C-major scale.

If a musician is playing over a section of a tune where the underlying chord is C major, then he will tend to pick notes from a C-major scale. When the chord changes, he will switch to a different scale appropriate to the new chord. (This, by the way, is also what the bassist is doing, simultaneously, underneath everything—picking a series of notes drawn from the scale associated with the chord that is in play for that stretch of the game board, as you can clearly hear bassist Jimmy Woode doing underneath Dizzy Gillespie's opening trumpet choruses on "U.M.M.G.")

So an up-tempo performance such as that of "The Eternal Triangle" can be seen, on one level, as an extended test of musical knowledge and coordination in which the players are demonstrating at high speed their understanding of the tune's harmonic structure and the many possible ways to negotiate the slalom course of the tune's succession of chords and implied scales.

Now, an important caveat: It is important to know that what I wrote in the three paragraphs immediately preceding is only half true at best. First, the whole truth is that each chord really implies *several* different scales, not just one, and an awareness of the ambiguous harmonic implications of each chord is part of what makes an interesting improviser interesting. But one of those scales will tend to exert the strongest claim on the music at any given time, for various reasons, so to keep things simple—for now, at least—let's consider only the most common scale implied by each chord.

Second, it is important to remember that no interesting musician conceives of improvisation as a process of shuffling scales simply to illustrate, or conform to, a harmonic pattern—that would be boring for everyone concerned. The ability to do that provides the players with a set of raw materials without which the musicians couldn't play together intelligibly, a set of ground rules. But without a few other elements in the mix to create interest, for player and listener alike, the activity would be mechanical and ultimately pointless.

•   •   •

One thing that allows musicians to fashion something more interesting than a mere series of scales on top of chords is what one can call "melodic imagination." Melody is an element that combines harmony and rhythm, but it is more than just the sum of the two elements; there are quite a few improvisers who have mastery over harmonic complexity and rhythmic variation but who don't think primarily in melodic terms.

Melodic imagination is difficult to define. Its products are roughly equivalent to "ideas" or "concepts" in discourse. We all know the type of conversation in which we are trading familiar notions and phrases back and forth, making small talk, reheating and serving up phrases we have heard others use—barroom or cocktail party conversation. Sometimes that kind of talk can be animated and enjoyable. But most of us know the difference between that kind of conversational mode and the moment when we have an "idea"—when we put things together for ourselves in a new way, when we come up with something that hadn't been there before, instead of just rearranging what was already there. This is an analogy for what the melodic imagination does.

Some musicians' most characteristic mode of thinking is in "sequences"—series of phrases in quick succession that have the same, or very similar, rhythmic outline, but that begin on different notes of the scale. You can hear Sonny Stitt do this throughout "The Eternal Triangle." Often it is done for a percussive effect, and it is primarily a rhythmic device, although it is often used to make a point about the harmony as well. Almost all jazz musicians use sequences in their playing at least occasionally; if nothing else, it is a way of communicating directly with the drums. Rhythmic patterns can be set up by a soloist through sequences that can either echo patterns that the drummer is playing or create counter-rhythms.

Other musicians place more of a premium on coming up with phrases that function in a somewhat different way. Listen, for example, to the way Wayne Shorter enters his sax solo on "Footprints," at around 4:20. Before him, Miles Davis has played essentially a series of rhythmic shapes, a fantastic dance, involved intimately with the rhythm. Shorter, by contrast, enters with a meditative, asymmetrical idea that almost floats above the rhythm, and as he gets into his solo, he continues to play a series of interesting and unexpected melodic ideas, sometimes directly addressing what the rhythm section is playing, and sometimes deliberately seeming to hover above it. But at 5:26 he gets interested in a sequence, an oddly shaped one with its roots in something he played at around 5:16; this new sequence lasts a few bars until, at around 5:30, it mutates into another sequence that he plays around with until about 5:47. The difference between this latter material and the material he plays at the beginning of his solo points to the difference between nonmelodic imagination and melodic imagination.

On "The Eternal Triangle," we can witness a fascinating match between Sonny Stitt, who is essentially a sequence player, manipulating scales and rhythmic patterns in an almost endless variety, which made him one of the greatest practitioners of this technique in the history of jazz, and Sonny Rollins, whose playing consists of almost nothing but "ideas," or at least it did at the time of this recording. The "sequence" approach is so much a part of the grammar of Stitt's playing that it is almost pointless to single out individual examples. One classic example, though, is a stretch in his solo between 3:18 and 3:25. If you keep listening beyond that point, you will hear how he seamlessly slides from his characteristic scale-pattern-based improvisation into another sequential passage between 3:34 and 3:38. But he does this kind of thing throughout. The swinging momentum that he generates is thrilling; Stitt integrated this technique into his conception so thoroughly that when he is playing at his best, as he is here, it doesn't feel formulaic.

Sonny Rollins is a different type of player altogether. One gets the feeling that he would rather bleed than play patterns or repeat himself. When he uses sequences, they tend to be toward a humorous, or even sarcastic, effect. This is one reason why his meeting with Stitt is so fascinating, even from a dramatic perspective. Both are great players, both at the top of their game, yet they represent, in a sense, different philosophies—Stitt the endless inventiveness in rearranging the scale patterns suggested by the chord progression, the constant recombining of familiar building blocks into yet another reaffirmation of mastery over the known facts; Rollins the creative imagination that constantly desires not just to dominate the facts but to create new facts, to create an arena for the emergence of surprise, contradictions, fresh logic.

Of course, things aren't quite that simple when you are listening to musicians of this caliber. For a startling example, listen to the rapid-fire four-bar exchanges between Stitt and Rollins on "The Eternal Triangle," beginning right around 6:21. The tempo is so rapid that each four-bar statement takes about three seconds. To keep things as clear as possible, we can look at this step-by-step.

6:21: Rollins leads off.
6:24: Stitt answers.
6:27: Rollins plays an ingenious, swinging four-bar passage, to which . . .
6:30: Stitt responds with a series of beautifully peeled-off and symmetrical sequences.

6:33: Rollins comes up with another very unusual and fresh melodic figure.

6:36: Stitt responds with another sequential series of scalar passages.

6:39: Now Rollins decides to play a sequence of his own, in a kind of jabbing, sarcastic echo of the sequence Stitt just played.

6:43: Stitt's response pointedly avoids sequences; his four bars end, in fact, with a very nice melodic phrase.

6:46: A new chorus begins; Rollins plays four bars of relatively smooth—even Stitt-like—eighth notes.

6:49: Stitt responds, opening with an asymmetrical phrase not unlike something Rollins would play.

6:52: Rollins, perhaps hearing a subtle implied challenge in Stitt's little asymmetrical phrase, begins his four bars with a mocking nursery-rhyme phrase.

6:55: Stitt throws Rollins's nursery phrase back at him, playing it out in a series of scalar sequences, and now things are starting to get real interesting.

6:59: Rollins enters the tune's bridge, or B part, with a Stitt-like scalar passage, humorously slowing the notes and displacing the tempo in the third and fourth bars.

7:02: Stitt brilliantly counters with an even more interesting rhythmic displacement in his own sequence.

7:05: Rollins goes into the final eight bars of the chorus again, with his own version of a Stitt-like sequence, staggered, asymmetrical, and aggressive, to which . . .

7:08: Stitt responds with a direct repetition of the phrase Rollins just played, turning it into a series of descending sequences. . . .

And on they go into a new chorus, and on and on. (Note: In the chorus, beginning at 7:37, they switch from four-bar exchanges to eight-bar exchanges, continuing with the "eights" for the rest of their dialogue.)

It is a great example, one of the very greatest ever recorded in fact, of two musicians speaking the same language at such a high level of skill at such a pitched level of alertness for such an extended time. And although it can be a cliché to compare artists and athletes, it may be appropriate here; one can think of this meeting as resembling the early-1970s boxing matches between Joe Frazier and Muhammad Ali. Frazier was one of the greatest craftsmen in the history of boxing, so great that his ability transcended mere craft, and Ali was a genius who lived to find fresh solutions to old problems. Among jazz aficionados there is no consensus about who "won" this particular bout; in fact, the more one listens to it, the more of a draw it becomes.

Remember, too, that the membrane between these two tendencies in playing is extremely porous; as we hear on "The Eternal Triangle," the same musician can and will use both types of imagination. But it might be said that a true melodic imagination is a rarer thing, even among excellent and important jazz musicians, than even a highly developed harmonic and rhythmic faculty.

∿∿∿

It should also be said that not all jazz improvising, even on chorus-type tunes, conforms to the "chord changes" model. Another approach was used most famously and influentially by Miles Davis and his sextet in the very well-known 1959 album *Kind of Blue* (Columbia/Legacy), but it was also used by other musicians before, including Jelly Roll Morton and Charles Mingus. In it, instead of negotiating a harmonic obstacle course or steeplechase, musicians play over a single scale, or "mode," for a much longer stretch of the game board; the harmony stays static, in that sense, rather than "progressing." One scale will give way to another periodically, for variety, but the understructure doesn't consist of a series of harmonic pushes and pulls, momentary resting places and ladders and slides. The challenge is to find something interesting to say without having this scaffolding of chord progression to offer patterns.

This approach, usually referred to as the "modal" approach, became perhaps the dominant way of playing jazz for young musicians who grew up in the 1960s and 1970s. It was felt to be very freeing for those who had come to feel trapped in the chord-changes approach. The "trap" in the chord-changes approach had always been that a musician could get obsessed with the "means"—the quasi-mathematical wonderland of chords and scales and their endless permutations—at the expense of the "ends," which have to do with expression, with real inventiveness over and above a fascination with the nuts and bolts themselves. A musician might say dismissively of another that he was merely "running the changes" rather than coming up with something representing an individual point of view. The modal approach eliminated most of that externally imposed "story line," and challenged musicians to come up with something interesting that was based on a looser, less "determined" set of coordinates.

"Footprints," like so much of Miles Davis's work in the 1960s and after, largely follows a modal approach. While a 12-bar blues in form, "Footprints" doesn't follow a conventional pattern of blues chord changes; instead, the musicians play off of two or three modes, resembling minor-key scales, and the effect is a kind of suspension, a feeling of being in a room where things are happening around you, rather than going down a track where things happen in a predictable order. The modal approach, because it tends to eliminate the kinds of tensions that chords set up to pull you through the music, also undercuts, in a sense, the feeling of moving forward through time, of harmonic cause and effect. At its best, it is an extremely refreshing alternative to all that potentially obsessive causality.

Of course, the modal approach came to have its own clichés, to suggest its own mechanical solutions. Some players ended up playing endless mechanical sequences anyway, only over static harmonic backgrounds rather than shifting, chord-changes-type landscapes. Without an extraordinarily fertile melodic imagination, one can run out of ideas very quickly, playing over a single scale; chord changes, at least, offer prods to the imagination, a succession of new facts to spur new variation. What seemed to get revealed after years of the dominance of the modal approach was the rarity of superabundant melodic imagination among musicians. So this approach, which initially seemed to be a means by which to exercise and challenge the melodic imagination, eventually pushed musicians toward other values—texture, dynamics, intricacy, intensity of rhythmic patterning, and so on.

~~~

Alto saxophonist and composer Ornette Coleman offered yet another approach to these questions when he arrived on the scene at the end of the 1950s. In effect, he proposed abandoning any predetermined harmonic template, along with standard chorus forms. Instead, the *melodic* imaginations of the players would be what determined the direction of the music. His music wasn't

atonal, exactly; in fact, Coleman's music almost always sounds tonal. It was just that the implied harmonic landscape was determined at any given moment by the implications of the soloist's improvised melodic line, rather than the melodic line being guided by a harmonic map.

Significantly, the classic Coleman Quartet on his most influential early recordings, for the Atlantic label, had no piano; it consisted only of Coleman's alto, Don Cherry's trumpet, Charlie Haden on bass, and either Ed Blackwell or Billy Higgins on drums. The piano tends to function as a kind of harmonic superego, and the kinds of chordal responses most pianists would have generated at that time would have been too harmonically determining of the direction of the music.

In any case, to be able to play in this setting, all the members of the group needed to be extremely alert to the implications of what the lead voice was playing, and the lead player needed to be alert to what the others were playing; there was no way to go on autopilot. The whole point, in a sense, was to render autopilot nonoperational.

⁓⁓⁓

The third element mentioned at the beginning of this chapter, the rhythmic resources available to the improvising musician, has been touched on only glancingly so far. It is probably obvious already that rhythm and harmony are intimately related, especially in jazz, where the essentially percussive nature of much melodic invention is, to a large extent, a defining element of the music. But the questions suggested by that relationship open up further questions about the nature of time itself, in music, and they need a chapter of their own, which is coming up next.

Further Listening:

Improvisation

Most of the recordings already mentioned in the "Further Listen-ing" sections of previous chapters are full of great improvisation and can serve as illustrations of this chapter's points as well. How-ever, when you're trying to hear the way a musician uses the under-lying harmonic structure of a given tune to make improvised variations, it may be helpful to listen to performances of songs you already know. That way, the melody is already in your mind and can sort of lurk under the succesive improvisations. Also useful are recordings where the melody is stated very clearly to start off with.

A good place to start is Billie Holiday's 1938 recording of "When You're Smiling" (Columbia/Legacy). This is a helpful recording even for those who don't already know the song, since the performance begins with a very straight rendition of the melody from Benny Mor-ton's trombone. In the second chorus, Billie Holiday sings the melody, making her own slight variations on it, altering it here and there as she pleases but still recognizably following the melody. Then there are two completely improvised solo choruses, the first from pianist Teddy Wilson and the second from tenor saxophonist Lester Young. Young's solo is almost a full chorus of amazing inven-tion; because of what has come before, you can hear immediately how his fresh melodic lines follow the contours of the song's under-structure without actually quoting from the melody.

Another great Billie Holiday recording for this purpose is the much less familiar "Me, Myself, and I," (Columbia/Legacy. Note: Two takes were recorded, following the same routine; take 1 is, in my opinion, the better of the two). Here, after a four-bar introduction by Lester Young, Billie Holiday sings the melody—a classic AABA pop ditty of the time. Then there is an improvised chorus split up among Edmond Hall's clarinet, Buck Clayton's trumpet, and James Sherman's piano. Then the real magic happens: Holiday comes back in for another chorus, singing the melody, but this time backed up by Lester Young's tenor, which cajoles and comments, twines and dances around her vocal; the singer is plainly exhilarated and sings to the hilt. In one fused moment, we have the melody and a fantastic improvisation on the harmonic structure, and one wants it to go on forever. Sometimes it is hard to believe that beauty and sympathy like this can actually exist, but luckily, we have the recorded proof.

One more vocal performance that might be singled out from among the countless good examples available is Dinah Washington's 10-minute-long live up-tempo version of "Lover, Come Back to Me," from the album *Dinah Jams* (Emarcy). Here the great jazz singer plays it straight for a first vocal chorus, then makes way for a succession of solos by various good and great musicians of that time, most especially the trumpeters Clark Terry, Maynard Ferguson, and Clifford Brown. You can feel the temperature rise in the room as the track goes along, and her final vocal chorus is a shouted abstract of the melody, with the musicians improvising behind her in a terrific, roaring finish.

~~~

Another way of approaching hearing the harmonic understructure through improvised variations is to listen to various artists' recordings of the same song. There are plenty of songs that have been recorded many times throughout the history of jazz. A good choice would be the ballad "Body and Soul," which, in addition to being the beneficiary of one of the greatest and most famous improvised solos in the history of recorded jazz, by Coleman Hawkins, has been recorded by many major jazz musicians. Following are some landmark performances.

A good place to start might be Louis Armstrong's 1930 recording (Columbia/Legacy), in which Armstrong plays it pretty close to straight in his muted opening solo, and there's a very straight, Guy Lombardo–like passage from the saxophones as well. Then Armstrong comes in with his vocal, which bends and smears and pulls the melody all over the place to great expressive effect. Billie Holiday's 1940 recording (Columbia/Legacy) is, of course, excellent as well.

But after you have learned how the melody sounds played or sung straight, tenor saxophonist Coleman Hawkins's 1939 reinvention of the song (RCA/BMG) will be a revelation. After only the briefest nod to the melody at the outset, Hawkins takes off on a purely improvised set of variations on the underlying harmony that caused a sensation and became an instant classic. Hawkins's powers of invention are so strong that he actually makes a new composition on the framework of the old, which is in some ways the highest goal of jazz improvisation. His thoughts are so cogent that words have even been put to his improvised solo; vocalist Eddie Jefferson's recording (Prestige) will be fun for anyone who knows the Hawkins recording—and anyone interested in jazz must come to know the Coleman Hawkins recording of "Body and Soul."

Sonny Rollins's unaccompanied solo version (Verve) is oddly lacking in tension or direction, but John Coltrane's inspired 1960 rendition (Atlantic) is one of the great ones. Among other things, Coltrane reharmonized sections of the song, giving it a very different flavor in spots, and those new "changes" became standard on performances of the tune. Interestingly, tenor saxophonist Dexter Gordon, one of the main influences on Coltrane's development, himself used Coltrane's arrangement of the song when he recorded it in 1970 on his album *The Panther* (Prestige).

A few other versions that should be mentioned—again, among many worthy recorded performances—are two very different 1961 solo performances by Thelonious Monk, recorded live in Europe (Riverside), on both of which Monk applies his own unmistakable sensibility to the tune and recasts it as a Monk composition; piano genius Art Tatum's fantastic 1950s solo version (Pablo); and a masterpiece by alto saxophonist Lee Konitz, retitled "Figure and Spirit." Recorded for Progressive Records, this sprawling, amazingly sensitive and imaginative performance is tough to find but worth whatever it takes.

~~~

On the other hand, it can also be instructive to hear one extremely inventive improviser play multiple versions of the same song. One of the most inventive improvisers who ever lived was altoist Charlie "Bird" Parker. When he came along, in the 1940s, he almost single-handedly rewrote the grammar book for improvisers, lending new ways of linking scales together and negotiating the harmonic courses presented by the popular tunes favored among the jazz musicians of the time. Bird's mind was so fertile that almost every scrap of music he played into a microphone has been issued and reissued countless times, even badly recorded live performances and broadcasts.

In the recording studio, Bird would often record multiple takes of the same tune, coming up with radically different improvisational strategies on the same material each time. Comparing these take by take can be extremely instructive for anyone deeply interested in jazz improvisation. Plus, they are great listening. His late-1940s recordings for the Dial and Savoy labels have been issued so that you can hear the various takes of tunes like "Ornithology," "Now's the Time," "Embraceable You," "A Night in Tunisia," and "Donna Lee" in succession, with a supporting cast including stars and stars-to-be such as Miles Davis and Bud Powell; likewise his recordings for Norman Granz's Clef Records and associated labels in the early 1950s, later absorbed into the Verve catalog and available as *Bird: The Complete Charlie Parker on Verve*. All of it will reward close listening.

One song that Parker particularly liked to improvise on was Ray Noble's "Cherokee," of which there are quite a few Parker versions, both official and unofficial. There are three to pay special attention to. The first is an early version on the disc *The Complete Birth of the Bebop* (Stash), recorded in 1942, before Bird had made his big splash, with only rhythm-guitar and very light drum backing. He plays the melody straight for the first eight bars, then begins a great series of improvisations in which you can hear his style mutating from its Lester Young–inspired base into what it would become. It has the thrill of discovery about it. Three years later, in 1945, he would record one of his most celebrated performances, the blazing "KoKo" (Savoy), a startling, utterly amazing improvisation on the chords of "Cherokee" that is one of the definitive jazz performances on record. Earlier that same day in the studio, the recording microphones captured Bird running through "Cherokee" at a more modest but still daunting tempo, and that track, which they titled "Warmin' Up a Riff," is also terrifically inventive. At one point you can hear Dizzy Gillespie, who is playing piano behind Parker for this warm-up, laugh out loud in surprise and delight at a brilliant turn of phrase that Bird makes.

As previously stated, there are many recordings you can find of familiar tunes recast by jazz musicians, and no room to exhaustively list them. One musician who liked to record recognizable, pretty tunes was Miles Davis. His simple and delicious recording of "Bye Bye Blackbird" (the version on 'Round About Midnight, Columbia/Legacy), with John Coltrane on tenor, is a nice set of moody, subdued variations over a structure that most listeners will recognize without even thinking about it. The same might be said for his excellent versions of "Someday My Prince Will Come," "Summertime," and "My Funny Valentine" (all Columbia), and "The Surrey with the Fringe on Top" (Prestige).

Another master musician who loves to indulge a taste for well-known tunes that rarely get the jazz treatment is Sonny Rollins. In addition to his own version of "The Surrey with the Fringe on Top" (Blue Note), he has recorded versions of "There's No Business Like Show Business" (Prestige), "When You Wish upon a Star" (RCA/BMG), "Toot Toot Tootsie," "Till There Was You" (both Riverside), "Wagon Wheels," "I'm an Old Cowhand," and even "Rock-A-Bye Your Baby with a Dixie Melody" (Contemporary), to name some of the more outre ones. He delivers them with a completely characteristic combination of loving affection and sardonic mockery. Later in his career he continued this predilection, at one point recording Stevie Wonder's "Isn't She Lovely?" (Milestone), among other unexpected picks. He also loves to play calypsos, the simple melodies and chord progressions of which make their structure especially accessible for nonmusicians to follow during the improvisations. Aside from his own "St. Thomas" (Prestige), "Don't Stop the Carnival" (versions on RCA/BMG and Milestone), "The Everywhere Calypso," and "Duke of Iron" (Milestone), his versions of the calypso standards "Brownskin Girl" (RCA/BMG) and "Hold 'Em Joe" (Impulse) are super-infectious and enjoyable.

Although he gained a deserved reputation as a leader of the 1960s avant-garde, John Coltrane also had an ear for simple popular tunes that could be turned to his purposes. By far the most well-known performance of one of these, and one of the most popular jazz recordings of all time, is his 1960 version of "My Favorite Things" (Atlantic). Coltrane converts the tune (from the score of *The Sound of Music*) into a churning, hypnotic chant, with his soprano saxophone doing wonders over the decidedly modal approach taken by the rhythm section. He gave a similarly incantatory treatment to a tune from *Mary Poppins*, "Chim Chim Cheree," on his 1965 album *The John Coltrane Quartet Plays* (Impulse); to the very well-known "Summertime," on the Atlantic disc *My Favorite Things*; and to "Greensleeves," on *Africa/Brass* (Impulse).

~~~

One of the reasons Coltrane liked the particular songs just mentioned, and played them so much, was that in each of them the harmonic understructure stays relatively simple and, in places, almost static for sizable stretches of the form. They gave him plenty of room, so he wasn't crowded by a succession of chord changes. Coltrane, who played in the Davis band on *Kind of Blue*, had been liberated in some ways by what he learned about "modal" playing, and he went on to explore the modal technique to its furthest reaches.

The irony, if it is an irony, is that Coltrane had also been in some respects the ultimate chord-changes player; the style of playing over chord changes that he evolved in the late 1950s was dubbed "sheets of sound" by critic Ira Gitler because of Coltrane's super-rapid way of trying to play every possible permutation of every chord and scale as it passed. After a certain point, it seemed as if Coltrane wasn't getting enough density, wasn't able to challenge himself enough, and he wrote his own tunes in the late 1950s, such as "Giant Steps" (Atlantic) and "Moment's Notice" (Blue Note), that had harmonic understructures in which the chords changed faster than in any conventional tune then being played, as well as having unusual relationships that broke with some of the standard grammar for the transfer from chord to chord. It was almost as if in trying so hard to scratch every remaining itch of chord-changes-based structure, what he was really trying to do was free himself from the chords in the first place.

Perhaps it was a relief to him for a while to know that he didn't have to constantly be chasing those chord changes around the board. In the 1960s he continued to find ways of escaping from any form of harmonic gravity at all.

The justly famous 1959 Miles Davis album *Kind of Blue* (Columbia/Legacy) contains some of the most beautiful playing in recorded jazz, and it has been written about so extensively that there is probably not much need to dwell on it. There was a freshness in the studio for these musicians, and for a while, at least, the looseness of the harmonic garments they wore during these sessions gave them a freedom that occasioned some of the best playing any of them ever did. "So What" is the best-known track from the disc, but the other tracks—"Freddie Freeloader," "Blue in Green," "All Blues," and "Flamenco Sketches"—all use the approach and, taken together, add up to one of the cornerstones of any jazz collection.

Kind of Blue was not, however, the birth of modal jazz, as some seem to believe, although it doubtless did more than any other recording to popularize the approach. Charles Mingus's 1957 album *Pithecanthropus Erectus* (Atlantic), while hardly the fully re-alized, charismatic, complete statement that *Kind of Blue* is, contains long modal stretches on the title track as well as on the 15-minute "Love Chant," which incorporates both standard chord-changes and modal sections. The sound quality is a little stark, or over-present, as it sometimes is on Atlantic jazz recordings from the late 1950s, but there is fine playing here not only from Mingus but also from alto saxophonist Jackie McLean (who was a great chord-changes player but also became a devotee of modal playing in the 1960s) and the little-known but excellent J. R. Monterose on tenor sax.

If one wanted to go even further back for examples of modal playing, one could go all the way to 1927 for Jelly Roll Morton's "Jungle Blues" (RCA/BMG), a startling thing if you've never heard it before, or even if you have—a series of solos over a throbbing pulse and a static, single chord, pounded out repeatedly, with just the smallest harmonic genuflection at the end of each chorus in the direction of tension and resolution.

~~~

Ornette Coleman's quartet recordings for Atlantic with Don Cherry, Charlie Haden, and Billy Higgins or Ed Blackwell (*The Shape of Jazz to Come, Change of the Century, This Is Our Music, Ornette, The Art of the Improvisers*, et al; also available in a complete box set from Rhino entitled *Beauty Is a Rare Thing*) are classics and show both his unique style of improvising and the way that style plays out in a group context. In some slightly later recordings, he is the only horn and is accompanied by bassist David Izenzon and drummer Charles Moffett. The live recordings with this trio, such as *At the Golden Circle,* volumes 1 and 2 (Blue Note) and *Town Hall, 1962* (ESP), feature him in extended and very freewheeling performances that, I think, show his improvising at its most characteristic. In later years Coleman has written compositions for large orchestra, played with electric bands, and even made some excellent recordings with pianists such as Geri Allen and Joachim Kuhn. The disc with Kuhn, recorded live in Leipzig and titled *Colors* (Harmolodic/Verve), is to my ears the closest thing to his great *Town Hall, 1962* performance that Coleman has released in recent years; the performances range widely over all kinds of landscape, and Kuhn's piano is perfectly attuned to Coleman's polymorphous approach.

King Oliver's Creole Jazz Band in Chicago, 1923. From left: Honore Dutrey, trombone; Baby Dodds, drums; King Oliver, cornet; Louis Armstrong, slide cornet; Lil Hardin, piano; Bill Johnson, banjo and bass; Johnny Dodds, clarinet. Photograph courtesy of the Frank Driggs Collection.

Five

Swing, Rhythm, Time, Space

1

Separately, some of these same observations—about form, about harmonic structure, about blues, about the relation of foreground to background—might apply to music nobody would call jazz. Bluegrass music uses blue notes and has solo improvisation; classic rock-and-roll bands have rhythm sections, and their music is often based on the blues; Broadway show-tune cabarets present popular standards by Gershwin and Rodgers & Hart and Cole Porter, as jazz musicians do. It is the combination of these, and other, elements—in varying measure—that has everything to do with making the music jazz.

In fact, jazz is marked above all by dynamic tension among disparate elements. It is certainly not the only musical form of which this might be said, but in jazz, to a high degree, that tension is what the performance is "about." A successful jazz performance presents a very specific kind of unity, almost a paradox, in which on every level—harmonic, rhythmic, stylistic, and so on—the elements of the performance pull against one another and create a tension that gives the performance its unique qualities.

Partly this is because, as was said earlier in this book, a jazz ensemble consists not just of different instruments but also of different sensibilities. This fact inflects every aspect of jazz performance and gives creative life to the specifically musical tensions that characterize jazz. And one of the main sets of tensions in a jazz performance has to do with the passage of time, the peculiar variable relations between movement and stasis, and among different kinds of time. That is what this chapter is about.

∿∿∿

We may as well start with the notoriously hard-to-define quality usually called "swing." Duke Ellington once wrote a song called "It Don't Mean a Thing If It Ain't Got That Swing," but even the most articulate jazz musicians have found it difficult to define what they mean by the word. On top of that, the question turns out to be controversial; some critics recently have maintained that swinging is not an integral element of jazz. But it can't be denied that this quality is present in the playing of almost every great soloist and ensemble in jazz history—from Louis Armstrong and King Oliver through Benny Goodman, Count Basie, Billie Holiday, and Duke Ellington, through Dizzy Gillespie, Charlie Parker, Stan Getz, and Miles Davis, through Charles Mingus, Thelonious Monk, John Coltrane, and Ornette Coleman. And no judgment is more final out of most jazz musicians' mouths than that of whether or not a group or a soloist is swinging.

Swing is an element that is, in fact, partly technically explainable. But it is also partly a matter of delivery of expressive elements that are beyond accurate description. It is, in this sense, like having a good accent when speaking a language. Some elements of proper pronunciation can be broken down and explained, but others eventually boil down to whether or not you have a good ear, can relax and focus, and are coordinated so that you can deliver sentences in a proper conversational cadence without hesitating infinitesimally in trying to shape your ideas, or remember the right word, or articulate unfamiliar syllables.

The true essence of the quality of swing is so hard to isolate and define that one is almost forced into metaphor and image. It might be best to start with the connotations of the word itself. Since "swing" is the word that has been used over the years to describe this extremely elusive quality, let us see what the image of an actual swing tells us.

Picture the arc of a common playground swing. Once you get into a regular rhythm on the swing, the amount of time it takes to get from one end of the arc to the other end and then back will be the same each time. But your actual speed as you traverse the arc is not constant; in fact, there is a curve of acceleration and deceleration—a speeding-up on the downward motion and a slowing on the upward part. As you approach the highest point, in either direction, the swing slows, slowing, slowing, and finally, there is a point of virtual weightlessness, then a moment of free fall as you swoop back down in the other direction.

Physical swing involves both the forward impetus of gravity on a falling object and the attrition of gravity on a rising object. The speed of the object as it moves is not constant but is subject to opposing forces that determine a varying curve of acceleration and deceleration. So there is a regularity in the "period" of the swing, but within that regular period there is a constant adjusting of the moving object's velocity. If we can picture a swing in which the speed is consistent from the top of one end of the arc to the top of the other, at which point there is an abrupt stop, then a reversal after which the swing goes in the other direction at a constant speed straight to the end of the arc . . . well, we wouldn't really call that a swing. There would be something mechanical and inorganic about it. This is one reason why metronomes, stopwatches, and digital clocks don't swing.

When you have a number of people who are swinging at the same time in a coordinated fashion—like, say, trapeze artists—the ability to simultaneously relax and yet also accurately gauge speed, distance, gravity, and the rest is absolutely crucial.

In a jazz performance, while every bar of music should take the same amount of "clock time"—fill the same "period"—within those bars and groups of bars there is a constant sense of respiration, of infinitesimal accelerations and decelerations in the actual playing, even though the background pulse, the tempo, remains constant. A large part of the music's meaning comes from this playing with time, this sense of being able to operate flexibly, accurately, and freely within the implied lockstep of chronology—an affirmation, in fact, of the living body against the dead abstraction of time.

For an example out of a million, one we saw in the previous chapter, listen again to the section of "The Eternal Triangle" from 6:59 to 7:02, where Sonny Rollins shifts from playing rapid eighth notes to quarter notes, and there is the sensation of suddenly slowing to half time even though the background rhythm remains constant. Miles Davis does this kind of thing constantly throughout his solo on "Footprints," even as the drummer, usually thought of as the timekeeper, does the same thing. Both trumpet and drum are aware of where they are in the form and in the pulse of the tune, yet they are able to imply different tempos, distort notes, and always meet up at the same place.

So swing is, first of all, organic. It is relaxed, free, yet precise. It is primarily physical, not abstract. It involves both acceleration and deceleration within a regular rhythmic context. We will keep this image of a swing in the backs of our minds as we ask some more questions.

〜〜〜

Part of that flexibility with regard to time involves a musician's ability to deliberately give each note a slightly different value, to hold some slightly longer, or cut others off slightly more abruptly. To do this precisely, not inadvertently, demands a very high level of control over one's instrument. You will notice that not all notes a musician plays are articulated equally, like machine-gun fire; instead, some are emphasized, or accented, more than others, just as we accent and shape syllables when we are speaking or singing.

In Jimmy Rushing's vocal on "Boogie Woogie," it is clear that not all the words he sings get the same stress or accenting. At around 0:52, listen to the way he sings the line "And I love to hear my baby call my name"; the words "And I" don't get the same emphasis as the words "love" and "call," for example. Likewise, in the next line the first two words, "She can," are a lead-up to the first really emphasized word, "call."

For an immediate parallel in instrumental playing, one can listen to almost any section of Sonny Rollins's solo on "Moritat." As with Rushing's vocal, the variety and texture of this solo has partly to do with the timing of the notes—where they are placed against the background rhythm—and partly with the articulation of the notes, analogous to the way your tongue and lips shape syllables as they come out of your mouth. This is true not just of the vocals and wind instruments but of the piano, the stringed instruments, even the drums. It is part of what musicians call "phrasing," which is also a part of swing.

The conductor Leonard Bernstein once brilliantly illustrated the importance of phrasing by contrasting a recording of the great blues singer Bessie Smith singing a verse of blues with a performance of the same lyrics and melody by an opera singer. The opera singer sang the same notes with the same note values, yet her delivery sounded inappropriately, even comically, stilted; it didn't swing. The small shadings, the subtle hesitations and accelerations and bendings of notes, that give the blues (and, by extension, jazz) its expressive character were not a part of her vocabulary.

~~~

Hand in hand with the way the tongue and lips (and fingers) shape the relations between the notes goes another, more quantifiable, element that has to do not so much with the way notes are shaped but with their placement in the beat, and even more, with the placement of accents on the notes.

As stated above, not all notes, even in a line of notes with the same rhythmic value, are given the same emphasis. To hear what I mean, read any sentence from this page aloud in a deliberate monotone, artificially giving every syllable exactly the same emphasis. Then read the same sentence aloud naturally, as you would ordinarily speak it. Immediately you'll notice that some syllables, some words, get accented more heavily than others, and that the accenting has something to do with how we understand the meaning of the sentence, just as the spoken sentence "I love you" will have a different sense depending on which word gets the emphasis.

We are all familiar with the concept that words have a mixture of strong and weak syllables. Poets and versifiers have always used this fact to create rhythmic patterns in verse. Think of:

> *The outlook wasn't brilliant for the Mudville Nine that day;*
> *The score stood four to two, with but one inning more to play . . .*

Or:

> *Shall I compare thee to a Summer's day?*
> *Thou art more lovely and more temperate . . .*

Or:

> *The wounded surgeon plies the steel*
> *That questions the distempered part . . .*

Or:

> *'Twas brillig, and the slithy toves*
> *Did gyre and gimble in the wabe . . .*

All of these excerpts, obviously from extremely different sources, are set to the same rhythm, what a poet or an English teacher would call "iambic meter." If one speaks the words with a natural inflection, every other syllable receives a heavy accent, in a regular pattern, and this pattern sets up a rhythm—ba-*DUM*, ba-*DUM*, ba-*DUM*, ba-*DUM* . . .

Poets use the natural accents occurring in words to create all kinds of rhythmic patterns, not just iambic—such as this triplet rhythm that the nonsense poet Edward Lear chose for a little self-portrait:

> *He sits in a beautiful parlour,*
> *With hundreds of books on the wall;*
> *He drinks a great deal of Marsala,*
> *But never gets tipsy at all.*

A jazz soloist uses this same principle—of varying the emphasis on different "syllables" within a line of musical notes—to achieve a desired rhythmic effect, and in order to communicate rhythmically with the other members of the group. This is such an integral part of jazz that we almost don't notice it unless a player *isn't* doing it.

Swinging is closely tied in with this technique of deliberately accenting certain notes in order to generate rhythmic patterns. Perhaps even more to the point, it is tied in with the very specific tensions that can be set up between those patterns and the regular tempo of the background rhythm. It is, in fact, the regular background pulse, whether stated or only implied, that gives coherence to the variations.

Listen again, for example, to all the rhythmic juggling going on in "The Eternal Triangle." All through this performance, the drums and bass are providing a steady, surging, constant pulse, while on top of it the saxophonists (and, later in the track, trumpeter Dizzy Gillespie) play counter-rhythms generated by accenting certain notes. One very clear example begins at 6:59, with Sonny Rollins and Sonny Stitt trading four-bar phrases back and forth, a section described in chapter 4. Another occurs later in the same track, during Rollins and Stitt's eight-bar exchanges; listen to Sonny Rollins's aggressively rhythmic way of punching and growling out notes, beginning at around 8:22 and continuing until the end of the saxophone exchanges, at 8:54 (Rollins is the heavier, rougher-toned player; his segments, during this passage, begin at 8:22, 8:36, and 8:48).

Even clearer are certain passages of Gillespie's playing on this track, where he plays the same note repeatedly purely for rhythmic effect, as if he were playing a drum, as, for example, from 10:11 to 10:16, or when he comes back in after Ray Bryant's piano solo, at 12:44.

But even when the soloists are not using such overtly percussive devices to create a rhythmic effect, they are still accenting notes in the middle of long lines of notes and setting up rhythmic patterns. All the musicians in an ensemble are listening constantly to what the others are playing, and are constantly responding to one another, rhythmically as well as harmonically. Jazz is, by its nature, "polyrhythmic"; its rhythmic character is determined by the play of varying overlapping rhythmic patterns against a regular underlying pulse, a layering of rhythmic levels.

This is true in all playing settings, not just the exciting up-tempo ones. A player or a group can swing at a fast tempo (such as "The Eternal Triangle"), or at a walking tempo (such as "Moritat"), or at a weightlessly slow tempo (such as "I Can't Get Started"); you can swing over a straight-ahead 4/4 meter, or a Latin rhythm, or even a waltz (3/4) tempo.

~~~

That being said, not every rhythmic pattern lends itself to swing, and some actually seem to undercut the feeling of swing—just as there are effective times to push our imaginary playground swing and other times when it would impede the swing's motion. You would push just as the swing began its downward arc away from you, to add to its momentum. You certainly wouldn't follow the swing and push it as it was approaching the far end of its arc— slowing toward the top and getting ready to come back toward you. In swing, timing is, literally, everything.

Similarly, there are specific ways of playing with the expectations set up by the regular rhythmic background of jazz, little rhythmic codes that are part of the idiom, patterns of accenting that work against the common 4/4 pulse in specific ways. Jazz musicians create variety, tension, surprise, and satisfaction in their playing by pulling away from that underlying rhythm, thereby creating a tension, and then meeting the underlying pulse again, satisfying it. Lagging behind, then catching up; feeling almost weightless for a moment, then letting gravity pull them back down; creating an alternate set of expectations to the underlying pulse, a set of counter-rhythms, and then varying those; all the while keeping that underlying pulse in mind, like a juggler. To have an entire group engaged in this same activity simultaneously takes a high level of mutual understanding and coordination, like the trapeze artists mentioned above.

That mutual understanding and coordination is possible largely because jazz musicians work with the same handful of counter-rhythmic building blocks, or patterns of accenting, which can be combined in almost infinite ways to make all kinds of complex rhythmic shapes. In this section, we will look at some of those building blocks.

First, though, let us look at the underlying pulse against which those building blocks function. If you tap your foot in a regular rhythm on the floor and count over and over, so that each number coincides with a tap of the foot, you will be counting out what musicians know as a 4/4 rhythm. Each group of four beats (divided here by a slash mark) makes up a bar of music, and each individual beat is called a quarter note. This pulse underlies most jazz.

For the purposes of hearing these building blocks, though, we will need to divide each of these quarter-note beats in half—into eighth notes. This is very easy to do; if you keep your foot tapping out that ONE-TWO-THREE-FOUR pattern, and now insert the word "and" between each number, you will have:

ONE and TWO and THREE and FOUR and / ONE and TWO and THREE and FOUR and / . . .

and so on. Now each of the four quarter notes is divided into two pulses—a "downbeat" (ONE, TWO, and so on) and an "upbeat" (and). We could divide each pulse into even smaller subdivisions, but this division into eighth notes will serve our purposes closely enough, and we will be able to look at the rough shape, at least, of a number of these building blocks.

The rhythmic building blocks to which we have been referring consist of short rhythmic patterns set on top of the underlying 4/4 pulse in specific places, and these patterns pull against that pulse to create a very fruitful tension. These patterns involve accenting specific combinations of downbeats and upbeats. To illustrate this, an accented beat will be shown in capital letters.

Note: The first five patterns shown below repeat every bar, over and over; for the sake of being able to better hear the way they work, they are illustrated twice in a row. The three patterns shown after these—6a, 6b, and 7—are compound patterns; it takes two bars to play the full pattern. In any case, all examples are shown over two bars, which are separated by a slash mark.

To hear these patterns, just keep that 4/4 beat going with your foot. You will be saying "one and two and three and four and" over and over, but you will put a heavy accent only on the capitalized beats. Or, if it is easier for you, clap your hands on the capitalized beats.

〰〰

One of the simplest examples, and the most basic to jazz's rhythmic character, is the little off-beat pattern that Jelly Roll Morton called the "Spanish tinge." This syncopated figure is found throughout not just jazz but almost all American vernacular music, including bluegrass, ragtime, and early rock and roll. It seems to have entered American music through New Orleans, imported as part of the African/Hispanic cultural heritage not only of African slaves but of the Latin and Caribbean cultures— Cuban, Mexican, West Indian, and so on—that inflected New Orleans music so profoundly.

This Spanish-tinge pattern itself has a number of infinitesimally slight variations, all of which could make a huge difference in the kind of dance they could inspire, but we can lay out the basic template as follows (start by tapping out the 4/4 pulse a couple of times to get the rhythm, and remember to accent, or clap on, the capitalized beats):

1. Simple Spanish tinge:

   ONE and two AND three and FOUR and / ONE and two AND three and FOUR and / . . .

You can hear Baby Dodds pecking out this Spanish-tinge rhythm on the woodblocks throughout "Weather Bird Rag," especially clearly from 0:07 to 0:14.

2. A Charleston rhythm can be formed merely by dropping the accent from the fourth beat of the Spanish-tinge pattern:

ONE and two AND three and four and / ONE and two AND three and four and / . . .

3. A variant:

ONE and two and three AND four and / ONE and two and three AND four and / . . .

This is what you will hear Carl Smith and Count Basie playing as their part of the little riff during the first two choruses of "Boogie Woogie."

4. Another variant, equally common:

one AND two and THREE and four and / one AND two and THREE and four and / . . .

5. And one more, slightly less common:

one and TWO and three AND four and / one and TWO and three AND four and / . . .

There are others, too; these are just five of the most common.

In each of these patterns, in practice, slight alterations are often made in the placement of the accents, especially the "and" accents; musicians will play them slightly before their appointed place, or in some cases slightly after. And as you can see, each one consists of a combination of accented downbeats and upbeats; against the even 4/4 pulse, an accented upbeat tends to create a rhythmic tension that is discharged by accenting a downbeat, just as inhaling implies the need to exhale as well. Remember this as we look at the following compound patterns.

~~~

All of the rhythms above have as their "period" one bar of 4/4 time. They are all written out twice in a row here to show them as patterns. But there are other patterns that are more complex, lasting for two bars to run their full course before repeating. Of these, by far the most common is a pair of two-bar patterns that Latin musicians call the "clave" (pronounced KLAH-vay), which means "key" (and is often played by the instrument of the same name). These clave patterns alternate one bar of Spanish tinge (ONE and two AND three and FOUR and . . .) with one bar of an insistent figure containing two accented downbeats (one and TWO and THREE and four and . . .).

6a. The first of the two clave patterns will sound familiar when you clap it out:

ONE and two AND three and FOUR and / one and TWO and THREE and four and / . . .

Years ago it used to be a catchphrase: "Shave and a haircut, two bits." It is also known universally to fans of rock and roll as a Bo Diddley beat, although Johnny Otis fans might think of it as the Hand Jive.

6b. The second of the two claves is just the reverse of the first one:

one and TWO and THREE and four and / ONE and two AND
three and FOUR and / . . .

These two, 6a and 6b, are the patterns that you will hear the clave sticks tapping out in much Cuban and other Latin music. It may not seem to make much difference which of the two halves starts things off, since the two bars just keep alternating, but in fact it makes a great difference in the rhythmic structure. In 6a, the "shave and a haircut" bar occupies all the odd-numbered bars of the performance (since it starts things off in the first bar and comes back in every other bar), and the "two bits" bar occupies all the even-numbered bars. In 6b, it is just the opposite. In other words, in 6a, the "shave and a haircut" bar is always the call, to which "two bits" is the response; in 6b, "two bits" is the call and "shave and a haircut" the response. And that will make all the difference in the kinds of rhythmic shapes that are suggested.

7. Another two-bar pattern has its roots in Brazilian samba music and will be familiar to all fans of the Brazilian-derived bossa-nova jazz popularized in the United States by Stan Getz and Antonio Carlos Jobim in the 1960s:

one and TWO and three AND four and / ONE and two AND
three and FOUR and / . . .

All these patterns are used—combined, recombined, switched around—by musicians both to add life and rhythmic coherence to longer lines of notes. Since all the musicians in the group know the same patterns, a saxophonist who plays, say, a "shave and a haircut" pattern in a line of eighth notes may be answered by a quick-eared bandmate with a "two bits" reply on the drums, and there are countless other possibilities for back-and-forth dialogue. The ideal, of course, is for musicians to have absorbed these patterns so deeply that they can truly "play" with them, setting up the expectations of knowledgeable bandmates, and listeners, by playing a pattern that they then subvert in a witty way, or extend in dialogue with someone else in the band. And if they can engage in that kind of play wittily and alertly, and in a relaxed and confident manner, along with the other members of a group, then they will probably at least be swinging, if nothing else.

These particular patterns tend to make music swing for reasons that may be suggested, again, by the image of a swing. If an upbeat tends to generate tension and a downbeat tends to discharge it, then it does make sense that optimal swing will be achieved by a combination of just the right number of accented downbeats and upbeats. If the main accents in the bars fall too often on the downbeats, then the music will feel lead-footed and devoid of interest. If the main accents fall only on upbeats (". . . and . . . and . . . and . . ."), so much tension will be generated that you will feel as if you can't catch your breath. Swinging consists of artfully timed buildup and discharge of tension.

And it is also important to remember that even these patterns will not swing if they are played mechanically or stiffly. These little patterns are here as a guide, an approximation. The rhythmic accents described are best thought of as being approached ever so slightly ahead of or behind the beat. To really get the proper feel, one would divide the bars at least into sixteenth notes, if not further. But even those divisions only approach the right timing; to deliver the timing exactly right is a matter not just of mechanically accurate placement in a measure but of articulating the note in the desired way, and ultimately, one needs to relax and listen. It is a combination of relaxation with alertness. In jazz, as in tennis or lovemaking or public speaking or boxing or any other activity that happens in real time, if you are alert and tense, you won't swing, and if you are relaxed and unfocused, you won't swing either.

∿∿∿

Here is one more thing to think about, for now, on this topic. If musicians are relaxed and alert (and technically accomplished and knowledgeable) enough, they can even play in several tempos at the same time.

Think of a typical 12-bar blues, of the type discussed in chapter 2, in which each of the 12 bars contains 4 quarter-note beats, as discussed just above. One full chorus (12 bars) of such a blues would contain 48 quarter-note beats ($12 \times 4 = 48$).

But if a musician is quick enough and has enough equilibrium, he could also think of the 48 beats in that chorus as divided into 16 bars of 3 quarter-note beats apiece ($16 \times 3 = 48$). So while his accompanists play 12 bars of blues in 4/4 time, the solo improviser could, if he could keep it straight in his mind, play 16 bars in waltz (3/4) time, over the same background, and at the end of the 48 beats, everyone would come out at the same place.

There are quite a few other ways of juggling time like this. And if you had a group in which the accompanists, too, were able to think and operate in these terms, then you would have something quite amazing.

There were in fact several groups who thought this way in the 1960s, and they raised group improvisation to new heights. Two of the greatest, if not the two greatest, of these were the John Coltrane Quartet, with McCoy Tyner on piano, Jimmy Garrison on bass, and Elvin Jones on drums; and the Miles Davis Quintet, with pianist Herbie Hancock, bassist Ron Carter, drummer Tony Williams, and either George Coleman or Wayne Shorter on saxophone. "Footprints" is an example of this Davis band at the height of its powers, bending, juggling, stretching, and even mocking the passage of time.

2

If the "subject" of photography is ultimately light itself, then what might the "subject" of music be? One could say "sound," but that would leave much out of the equation. Like the formulation about photography, it does leave out the peculiar ability of these sounds (or these light values) to move us emotionally and intellectually.

Photography, however, is different in that it has (at least in representational photography) a subject—people, landscape, objects—that also informs the image, just as narrative prose does. Music has no such external component toward which it points, unless we impose one upon it and say that it is about the planets, or the creation of the world, or a storm. Or it could always be about a dance—a bolero, a waltz, the Charleston.

Music depends not only on sound but also on the passage of time. In fact, music—at least tonal music, and most jazz is tonal—is almost completely *about* the passage of and the mastery over time. Time is what is being challenged and transfigured as a musician plays chorus after chorus on an up-tempo song, or as a rhythm section juggles and manipulates the underlying pulse as a soloist approaches the end of his allotted chorus on a ballad with tenderness and pathos, a small death every time. Although musical performance can be "timed," as the tracks are on the companion disc, musical performance—like a work of literature—is not really measured in clock time. Once a performance starts, the musicians and the listener move over to an alternate musical dimension in which time changes its very nature.

On the accompanying CD, it has been convenient to use clock-time markings to point to places in the performances for illustrative purposes. But if, during a performance, a listener (or a musician) becomes aware of the passage of actual clock time, something has very likely gone wrong in that performance. Clock time becomes irrelevant during an effective musical performance. To show what I mean, listen to any 20 seconds in King Oliver's "Weather Bird Rag" and then listen to any 20 seconds from the middle of Stan Getz's performance of "I Can't Get Started." Your clock will tell you that the same number of seconds has passed for both, yet how different that time feels.

It is not just a question of the tempo, although that is, of course, part of it. The performances of "Weather Bird Rag" and the Duke Ellington Orchestra's "U.M.M.G." are set at approximately the same tempos, but time feels different during the Oliver track than it does during Gillespie's opening solo on the Ellington track—just as the same half hour might feel very different in the middle of a crowded New Year's Eve party than it would in a car, alone, driving the first half hour of a long road trip on the way to the party.

The sense of time passing can also be affected by the length of the cyclical song form itself. If you compare "Boogie Woogie," in which each chorus takes about 16 seconds of clock time, with "Moritat," where each chorus takes roughly 46 seconds (toward the end, slightly longer because the quartet has slowed down ever so slightly), time feels different even though they are both set at about the same tempo. The revolving seasons of beginning, middle, and end come around more often in "Boogie Woogie," and you feel as if more ground has been covered.

The use of the term "ground" implies a different set of coordinates than temporal ones. The relations between time and space in music are ambiguous. We often experience time in tactile or physical terms. One can feel as if one has spent an enormous amount of time inside a very small time space, as if a moment or two have been stretched, opened up, to last a much longer time. The language we are forced to use in discussing time is itself physical, tactile: "stretching," "length of time," and so on. One of the deepest mysteries of music is that we can get the sensation of time slowing down, speeding up, changing shape—that a whole world can be conveyed in a three-minute performance, or a single moment of feeling extended over ten minutes.

Toward the end of his life, the rockabilly singer and guitarist Carl Perkins, who wrote the song "Blue Suede Shoes," sat down for an interview with me. At the end of our visit, I asked him a question that had been nagging at me. It had occurred to me that the two and a half minutes that Perkins spent recording "Blue Suede Shoes" on a particular day in 1955 had become thousands of hours of other people's lives. I had figured that based on the assumption that "Blue Suede Shoes" had sold a million copies (it had sold more). Say you could play the record twenty-five times in an hour. That meant you could play it a hundred times in four hours, and in forty hours, you could play it a thousand times. So it would take up forty thousand hours (238 weeks, or more than four and a half years) if everybody who bought the first million records played the record only once. And we know that they played it a lot more than that, and that it sold more than that. So those two and a half minutes out of his life had become years and years out of other people's lives, like the loaves and fishes in the Bible story. Had he ever thought about that?

Perkins looked at me almost as if I had given him bad or disturbing news, and he said, "No, I haven't. They could have . . . built a *city* in that amount of time. I don't know what to think about that."

I'm not sure that I do either, except that in a sense he did build a city; every creative artist does that through his or her imagination. One constructs a city of the mind and the soul, and then takes the listener on a trip through that city. It is a working model of reality. When one listens to a musical performance, one goes on a trip. But in jazz, unlike in European classical music, the musicians share a map but not a fixed itinerary, and so the audience shares their discoveries, adventures, and jokes at the same moment the musicians arrive at them.

The passage of time on that trip, and the relation of the individual sensibility to the passage of time, is always at the heart of the matter, the center of the frame. Not all jazz feels as if it is proceeding straight ahead down a track. Sometimes you are put in the middle of a room where things are happening all around you. On "Footprints," for example, sometimes it feels as if you are rushing forward headlong, and at other moments it feels as if time slows down and things are happening in slow motion. If "Footprints" is a city, sometimes you feel as if time is happening differently in different neighborhoods simultaneously.

Time is both abstract and palpable, a real oxymoron. It is ambiguous; it brings growth and increase, and it brings attrition and decay. In youth, time works for the body—making it grow, making it stronger and more coordinated, like the acceleration on the downward part of a swing's arc. After a certain invisible point is reached, time begins to work against the body, just as gravity does. Of course, if we measure time by the earth's orbit, its movement around the sun, the periods of day and night, the seasons, it might seem to be completely about the tension between gravity and momentum, and therefore about swing. The confrontation with those tensions, inside the finite span of a jazz performance, is a way of vanquishing time, but only for a time. This is a lesson that the music teaches over and over, from the jazz funerals of New Orleans to Stan Getz standing on the stage of Carnegie Hall dying of cancer, knowing that his days were numbered, and yet playing as if there were all the time in the world.

Every jazz performer—every artist—works, consciously or not, within this framework. Jazz musicians figure out a way to make an indelible space for themselves in time, within a world of attrition and decay. Their temporary victories over time stave off death by using the elements we have talked about so far in this book. When jazz is at its best and most important, these elements are combined in a way that is not just mechanical, not just about the elements themselves. They are there in the service of something a musician wants to express, which is nothing less than their individual sense of life. The next and final chapter will look at this most crucial, and most mysterious, aspect of jazz.

Further Listening:
Swing, Rhythm, Time, Space

Jazz musicians have swung differently in different eras; in some times and places the underlying pulse is much more strongly insisted upon than in others, for all kinds of reasons. Keep in mind that these qualities may be found equally in hundreds of other recordings, but if you want clear, concentrated examples of swinging, here are a few, from various eras.

We can start with the big bands of Count Basie and Benny Goodman, two of the most swinging of the swing era. Count Basie's band on the last couple of choruses of "Honeysuckle Rose" (Decca) achieves a transcendent, buoyant swing, each section solid and relaxed in its part. Other performances such as "One O'Clock Jump," "Jumpin' at the Woodside," and "Roseland Shuffle" (Decca) show the band's most swinging side, from 1937 and 1938. Their recordings of 1939 and 1940 are even lighter on their feet, and tracks such as "Clap Hands, Here Comes Charlie," "Taxi War Dance," and "Miss Thing" (Columbia/Legacy) are marvels of almost weightless propulsion. Goodman's band tended to be a bit more insistent on the downbeat, but the ensemble precision and strong swing are a pleasure to hear, almost seventy years later, in performances such as "House Hop," "King Porter Stomp," and "Sing, Sing, Sing" (RCA/BMG).

The prototype for Goodman's band (and, for that matter, for Basie's, at least at first) was the 1920s and early-1930s big band of Fletcher Henderson. The set *A Study in Frustration* (Columbia/Legacy) is a gold mine of fantastic performances; for one of the best examples of Henderson's band swinging at up-tempo, proceed directly to that set's "Yeah Man," an epic in riffs. To see how far the band had come since its beginnings, and also to see what Louis Armstrong brought to the band, a very instructive track is the same set's 1924 recording of "Shanghai Shuffle," which pokes along in the most unswinging manner until Armstrong's solo toward the end of the track, at which point everything takes off—for the duration of his solo. Single-handedly, Louis Armstrong was showing this band how to swing, and you can almost see the lightbulbs going on in everyone's head. Bennie Moten's Kansas City Orchestra was a powerhouse, and also the launching pad for Count Basie, who was the band's pianist. Their 1932 performance of "Toby" (RCA/BMG) outswings even Henderson's "Yeah Man," and has an apocalyptic quality to it, perhaps generated partly by the fact that the band was down to its last collective dime and its members almost literally starving when they arrived at the Camden, New Jersey, studio where it was recorded.

Duke Ellington represented a universally acknowledged peak of artistry and sophistication among big bands, along with amazingly compelling swing. The 1940 "Cotton Tail," featuring the mighty Ben Webster on tenor saxophone, along with a roaring series of choruses for a finale, and the 1942 "Main Stem" (both RCA/BMG) both show the Ellington band at its most swinging. During the 1950s and 1960s, Ellington continued to make astonishing recordings; for the purposes of this chapter, the album *Piano in the Background* (Columbia/Legacy) must be mentioned, along with the 1956 Newport Jazz Festival performance of

"Diminuendo and Crescendo in Blue" (Columbia/Legacy) and a medley version of "Kinda Dukish" and "Rockin' in Rhythm," recorded in Paris in 1963 (Atlantic), which must be heard to be believed.

Two big bands from the bebop era that placed a premium on swinging were those of Woody Herman and Dizzy Gillespie. Herman's most enduringly interesting band was probably his late-1940s Herd, as he called it, which was full of talent, especially in the saxophone section, which contained, at various times, Stan Getz, Zoot Sims, Al Cohn, and Serge Chaloff. Herman's recording of Jimmy Giuffre's "Four Brothers" (Columbia/Legacy) is a classic. Gillespie's late-1940s bands were roaring dynamos; tracks such as "Cool Breeze," "Oop-Pop-A-Da," "Stay on It," and "Jumpin' with Symphony Sid" are necessary to hear. Lionel Hampton's slightly earlier recordings of the wartime anthem "Flying Home" (Decca), one with tenor saxophonist Illinois Jacquet playing a much-copied solo, and another with Jacquet's fellow Texan Arnett Cobb, are also classics of big-band swing.

The annals of jazz recording are full of extremely swinging small-group performances, more than ever could be listed. But here is a small handful of definitive ones. Coleman Hawkins's 1937 European recording of "Crazy Rhythm" (Swing/DRG), with an all-star band that included alto saxophonist Benny Carter and Gypsy guitar genius Django Reinhardt, is a landmark of powerful swinging, as well as brilliant imagination. Pianist and singer Fats Waller led a small group throughout the 1930s that was one of the high-water marks of ensemble swing, powered largely by the leader's indomitable stride piano. Recordings like "Got a Bran' New Suit," "Christopher Columbus," "There Goes My Attraction," and "The Curse of an Aching Heart" (RCA/BMG) show Waller and his band to be among the all-time champions of swing.

The same could be said of violinist and vocalist Stuff Smith, a mainstay of New York's 52nd Street jazz scene in the 1930s. Recordings such as "I Hope Gabriel Likes My Music" (Columbia/Legacy) show him and his small band (which included trumpeter Jonah Jones) at their best. If you are motivated to find about as compact a definition of swinging as is possible, though, search out a short video clip of Stuff Smith playing a medium-tempo bounce blues along with the singer Big Joe Turner on the 1950s TV show *Jazz Party*. It is inserted without much fanfare in the middle of a very good documentary about a photograph, taken in Harlem in 1957, of an extraordinary gathering of jazz musicians, released as both *A Great Day in Harlem* and *The Great Jazz Day*. That one brief glimpse of Smith playing his two choruses will tell you everything about the nature of timing, inflection, touch, accenting, and spirit, and their relation to the ineffable quality of swing.

Finally, trumpeter Roy Eldridge was one of the most fiery and swinging musicians in the history of jazz. From his arrival on the scene in the 1930s, Eldridge commanded attention with his long, intelligent lines and his blistering-hot tone. Don't miss recordings such as "Warmin' Up," with a small band led by pianist Teddy Wilson (Columbia/Legacy), recordings under drummer Gene Krupa's leadership such as the small-band "Swing Is Here" (RCA/BMG) and the big-band classic "Let Me off Uptown" (Columbia/Legacy), and the 1937 tracks under Eldridge's own leadership, especially the two takes of "Wabash Stomp" (Columbia/Legacy), which crank the tension and swing up to an amazing pitch.

Any short list of recommendations from the post–World War II era would have to include Bud Powell's amazingly articulated and definitively swinging piano solos on "The Street Beat," "Ornithology," and "I'll Remember April," from a 1950 live session at Birdland that also included Charlie Parker and trumpeter Fats Navarro (various import labels), as well as his solos on "Wee" and "Hot House" from the 1953 *Jazz at Massey Hall* (Fantasy), on which he is alongside no less than Charlie Parker, Dizzy Gillespie, Charles Mingus, and drummer Max Roach.

Charlie Parker, as well as lending jazz a greatly expanded grammar, brought a new urgency to swinging lines of eighth and sixteenth notes; his late-1940s solos on "Dexterity," "The Hymn," "Big Foot," and most of his other recordings for the Dial label extend Lester Young's way of articulating eighth-note lines, and demonstrate his brilliant imagination as well. Parker's 1953 album *Now's the Time* (Verve) is one of the most consistently swinging sets of his playing available, especially the several takes of the medium-up-tempo blues "Chi-Chi," as is the 1950 live set *Bird at St. Nick's* (Fantasy), although the St. Nick's set has sound quality only a real Parker fan might want to sit still for. Altoist Jackie McLean was one of the foremost Parker disciples, and his album *Swing, Swang, Swingin'* (Blue Note) is cast in the mold of Parker's *Now's the Time*—alto saxophone and rhythm section playing plain, two-feet-on-the-floor bebop, mostly on standards like "I'll Take Romance" and "I Love You."

Some other standout recordings of the 1950s and 1960s appropriate to this chapter include the incendiary 1954 Art Blakey set *A Night at Birdland*, volumes 1 and 2 (Blue Note), featuring trumpeter Clifford Brown blazing his way through a live set of cooking bebop, blues, and ballads, alongside altoist Lou Donaldson and pianist Horace Silver. Everything on these discs is good and exciting, but Brownie outdoes even himself on "Wee Dot" and "Split Kick." You cannot swing harder than this, although Blakey tries, on his 1960 album *Roll Call* (Blue Note), with tenorist Hank Mobley and trumpeter Freddie Hubbard. Horace Silver's own quintet placed a heavy premium on this kind of heat; "Filthy McNasty," from *Doin' the Thing* (Blue Note), recorded live at the Village Gate, is an extremely buoyant performance that reaches way down into the funk as well.

Miles Davis's 1954 all-star recording of "Blue 'n' Boogie" (Prestige) contains very compelling playing not just from the leader but also from trombonist J. J. Johnson, Horace Silver, and, most especially, tenor saxophonist Lucky Thompson. Throughout, momentum is maintained by strategic use of riffs behind the soloists, and bassist Percy Heath and drummer Kenny Clarke cook hard. Pianist Wynton Kelly's presence in a rhythm section almost guaranteed a high swing level; his playing propels the exciting "No Blues" on guitarist Wes Montgomery's live 1965 set *Smokin' at the Half Note* (Verve). Other individual performances that could single-handedly illustrate swing at a surging tempo include Charles Mingus's riff blues "MDM" (Candid) and "E's Flat, Ah's Flat, Too" (Atlantic), Sonny Rollins's "Strode Rode" (Prestige), John Coltrane's wailing "Mr. PC" (Atlantic), Sonny Stitt's version of "I Never Knew" from *Personal Appearance* (Verve), and Ben Webster's solo on "Jive at Six" (Verve).

Swing can be absolutely relaxed and floating, as well as surging and propulsive. The critic Martin Williams once used Lester Young's final eight bars on his 1943 recording of "Sometimes I'm Happy" (Keynote) as an example of ultimate swing, delivered at a very relaxed walking tempo. Other good examples would have to include Bix Beiderbecke's solo on "Singing the Blues" with Frank Trumbauer (Columbia/Legacy), Count Basie's *misterioso* "Blues in the Dark" (Decca), "Pagin' the Devil" by the Kansas City Six with Lester Young (Commodore), Coleman Hawkins's 1944 "Sweet Lorraine" (Signature), both takes of Charlie Parker's 1947 interpretation of "Embraceable You" (Dial), Miles Davis's phrasing of Dave Brubeck's "In Your Own Sweet Way" (Prestige), Sonny Rollins's "You Don't Know What Love Is" (Prestige), "Port of Rico" by Illinois Jacquet (Verve), "Walkin' " by Miles Davis (Prestige—from the same session that produced "Blue and Boogie"), and Ornette Coleman's beautiful "Just for You" (Atlantic).

And as proof that it is possible to swing at a very slow tempo, a couple of quick examples: Ben Webster's smoldering, late-night blues "Soulville" (Verve); Miles Davis's ever so delicately maintained mood on "Blue in Green," from *Kind of Blue* (Columbia/ Legacy), which also features John Coltrane and pianist Bill Evans; and Charles Mingus's extraordinary "What Love" (Candid), on which Mingus steers a quartet of trumpeter Ted Curson, bass clarinetist Eric Dolphy, and drummer Dannie Richmond through a subtly shifting rhythmic landscape where the tempo curves from a slow walk to an almost suspended stillness, like a sleeper's breathing.

For the Spanish tinge and the claves used in various ways, a close listen to almost any jazz recording should provide plenty of examples. Some of the most exciting and interesting are recordings on which jazz players are placed in overtly Latin contexts, or in which they deal head-on with clave-based rhythmic backgrounds. There are many such performances in the annals of recorded jazz; here are a few standouts.

To hear Jelly Roll Morton himself demonstrate the Spanish tinge, listen to the amazingly coordinated playing on "The Crave" (Commodore), in which he plays all kinds of staggered rhythms in his right hand against his left hand's Spanish tinge. Another good example of Morton doing this is his performance of "New Orleans Blues" on *The Library of Congress Recordings,* volume 4 (Rounder).

It used to be standard to play a Spanish tinge, or rumba, beat under the minor-key strain of W. C. Handy's "St. Louis Blues," as you can very clearly hear Louis Armstrong's band do on his classic 1929 recording of that song (Columbia/Legacy). Armstrong also recorded the Cuban standard "The Peanut Vendor" (*"El Manisero"*) with his big band in the next year. Duke Ellington made full use of the Spanish tinge in his way all through his career; two of the most concentrated examples are the 1940 masterpieces "Conga Brava" and "The Flaming Sword" (RCA/BMG). Dizzy Gillespie had a life-long fascination with Latin rhythms and percussion. His late-1940s big-band recordings with the Cuban conga drummer Chano Pozo, including "Cubana Be," "Cubana Bop," and the explosive "Manteca" (RCA/BMG), are jazz classics, a fantastic fusion of bebop jazz with its rhythmic roots. There are also broadcast performances of this band available on various labels, as well as a great late-1950s live performance of "Manteca" from the Newport Jazz Festival (Verve).

Charlie Parker made several interesting recordings with the very popular Latin dance band led by Machito, including "Okiedoke" and "Mango Mangue" from 1948 (Verve). Bird's alto seemed to get fresh inspiration from the setting, and for a while he added Latin percussion to his own small groups, even recording some Latin favorites such as "La Cucaracha," "Tico Tico," and "La Paloma" with a small band, available as *South of the Border* (Verve). For a real treat, hunt down the May 1953 broadcast recordings from the nightclub Birdland, on which the great conga drummer Candido joins Parker's quartet for versions of tunes such as "Broadway," the blues "Cheryl," and a wild up-tempo "Moose the Mooche," generating terrific excitement (available on various import labels). Parker also liked calypsos, and there is a fantastic performance of him playing the calypso standard "Sly Mongoose" live at the Rockland Palace, available in various bootleg forms on various labels.

Sonny Rollins, too, loved to play calypsos, which also play rhythmically off of the Spanish tinge and allied patterns. He made many recordings of calypsos, of which some of the very best are "St. Thomas" (Prestige), "Hold 'Em Joe" (Impulse), "Brownskin Gal" (RCA/BMG), and "The Everywhere Calypso" (Milestone). Bud Powell made one of the most interesting and exciting bebop recordings using a Latin motif, the stunning 1951 trio performance of "Un Poco Loco" (Blue Note). Charles Mingus's album-long suite *Tijuana Moods* (RCA/BMG) takes the listener on a kaleidoscopic trip through the highs and lows of a Mexican sojourn and is not to be missed. The vibist Cal Tjader was a fine jazz player with deep roots in Latin music, and he recorded many albums with strong Latin rhythms throughout. Two of the most interesting from a jazz perspective are *Soul Sauce* (Verve), with its nice variety of grooves and a very strong performance of "Afro-Blue" featuring guitarist Kenny Burrell; and *Latin Kick* (Fantasy), a 1956 set that features the underappreciated tenor saxophonist Brew Moore.

For a while in the 1960s, the bossa nova—the fusion of jazz with Brazilian samba rhythms—became a craze. By far the best-known and biggest-selling of these Brazilian-based jazz recordings were those led by Stan Getz. The best of these may be *Jazz Samba* (Verve), a refreshing and delicious recording, also featuring guitarist Charlie Byrd. Another is *Getz/Gilberto* (Verve), which features not only the guitarist Joao Gilberto but also the pianist and composer Antonio Carlos Jobim. This set, by the way, is the source of the hit recording "The Girl from Ipanema," with its famous deadpan vocal by Astrud Gilberto, wife of the guitarist.

∿∿∿

While most jazz is played in 4/4 time, some musicians have made a specialty of playing in unusual meters. The most famous and popular of these is undoubtedly the pianist and composer Dave Brubeck, whose quartet with alto saxophonist Paul Desmond made some of the best-selling jazz records of all time. In addition to the hit "Take Five" (in which Desmond's sinuous alto leads the group through an engaging performance in 5/4 time), Brubeck played in waltz time and used all kinds of metric devices to bring a different flavor to jazz. His albums *Time Out* (which includes "Take Five"), *Time Further Out,* and several others have been packaged together by Columbia/Legacy in a multidisc set called *For All Time,* a feast for Brubeck fans.

Drummer Max Roach was fascinated with waltz tempo and made several recordings of waltzes. In addition to the classic track

"Valse Hot" (Prestige), recorded with Clifford Brown on trumpet and Sonny Rollins on tenor, Roach made the excellent album *Jazz in 3/4 Time* (Mercury), which also includes Rollins as well as trumpeter Kenny Dorham in a program of rhythmically fresh and invigorating compositions. And in the late 1960s the trumpeter Don Ellis made a specialty of leading a big band that played in sadistically complex time signatures, such as 7/4 and 19/4, and worse. His albums *Electric Bath* (Columbia/Legacy), *Live at Monterey*, and *Live in $\frac{3^{2}/_{3}}{4}$ Time* (Blue Note) stretch the ability of musicians to think in compound meters to its limit.

~~~

To hear musicians applying the kinds of techniques discussed toward the end of section 1 of this chapter, there is no better place to start than the recordings of Miles Davis's mid-1960s quintets. *'Four' and More* (Columbia/Legacy), recorded live at Philharmonic Hall in 1964, shows the leader along with saxophonist George Coleman, pianist Herbie Hancock, bassist Ron Carter, and the teenage drum phenomenon Tony Williams sliding in and out of time frameworks at will, thinking on several levels at once, maintaining tensions between competing frameworks almost to the breaking point. Astonishing examples abound where time seems to slow down and drift off, only to come back again at exactly the right spot, a multilevel chess game full of surprise and daring and an uncanny mix of focus and exhilaration among the players. One especially startling passage is Tony Williams's drum solo on "Walkin'," in which he seems to abandon the tempo altogether to play abstract figures over a static background—until at the very end he cues the band with a little figure and they pounce back in at exactly the original tempo and you realize that Williams was maintaining the pulse the whole time.

All of Davis's recordings of this period have moments of this type of magic (if not necessarily pitched to quite this level of intensity). Live sets such as *Live in Europe, My Funny Valentine* (both of these also featuring George Coleman on tenor), and *Miles in Tokyo* (with Sam Rivers replacing Coleman), and the great series of recordings with Wayne Shorter finally in place, including *ESP, Miles Smiles, Nefertiti, Sorcerer, Miles in Berlin,* and *Live at the Plugged Nickel* (all Columbia/Legacy), are landmarks of human intelligence, wit, and passion.

John Coltrane's classic quartet with McCoy Tyner, Jimmy Garrison, and Elvin Jones achieved almost the same level of rhythmic flexibility and coordination, spoken with a different accent, all centered around the leader's surging and fiery tenor saxophone. Records such as *Crescent, Coltrane, Live at Birdland, Africa/Brass, A Love Supreme, Impressions,* and *The John Coltrane Quartet Plays* (all Impulse) show Coltrane constantly suggesting multiple meters with his powerfully defined lines, and Elvin Jones (who was at least Tony Williams's equal for polyrhythmic subtlety and brilliance) matching him and goading him to even further explorations. Each of these sets is an adventure, to say the least.

And for another angle on the use of superimposed meters, investigate Ornette Coleman's *Free Jazz* (Atlantic), on which two different quartets play simultaneously in two different tempos, one twice as fast as the other, generating a pulsating and surprising sense of stasis. Coleman loved, and loves, to play melodies that seem to exist independently of an underlying tempo—one famous example being "Lonely Woman" from his seminal album *The Shape of Jazz to Come* (Atlantic). The bandleader Sun Ra was doing similar things a few years earlier than Coleman, as you can hear on his tune "Planet Earth" from the disc *Sound of Joy* (Delmark).

Stan Getz with Rufus Reid on bass, 1990. Photograph © Herb Snitzer.

Six

Telling a Story

1

This book has focused on more or less objective matters so far—on observable and quantifiable questions of technique, group organization, form, and so on. These are elements that we can point to and tote up in an attempt to ask what the elements are that might make up jazz.

~~~

Having technical command or knowledge is not necessarily the same thing as having something to say. Or you can say that having information is not the same thing as having a point of view about that information. Another way of putting it might be to say that knowledge is not the same thing as vision. Or imagination.

~~~

If the form and the harmonic progression of a given piece amount to a kind of narrative skeleton or story, as suggested in chapter 4, then each musician's improvisation amounts to a different version of the same facts, a retelling of the story but with different emphasis and sensibility, as in Akira Kurosawa's film *Rashomon*, in which several witnesses to the same events provide different accounts of "what happened." Each witness has a different story.

〰〰

Just as the literal image of a swing may be useful in thinking about the quality of swing in music, some elements of narrative technique in literature may be useful in discussing the way musicians approach improvisation.

Most jazz, with its emphasis on improvised solos, would seem, in literary terms, to be narrated in the first person. The very distinct and recognizable individual voice of the soloist inflects the material and makes that teller's version of the story distinct from anyone else's. Sonny Rollins would tell the "story" of "I Can't Get Started" in a manner very different from Stan Getz's; John Coltrane would tell it differently from their versions, as would Coleman Hawkins and Lester Young and Joe Henderson and Wayne Shorter and Ben Webster, to speak only of tenor saxophonists. It is the advancement of a personal tale told through the vehicle of a preexisting narrative skeleton.

By contrast, a performance such as King Oliver's "Weather Bird Rag" seems to be "narrated" less by an "I" and more by a "we"— less like *The Catcher in the Rye*, say, and more like *Our Town*. The point is not so much the spinning out of an individual sensibility as the construction of a group sensibility—composed, to be sure, of individualized voices. The story is, in a sense, more about how voices work together than about how they distinguish themselves one from the other.

It might be tempting to say the same about "Footprints," except there is such a high level of individuation among the voices, and such a high level of tension among them, that it is more like a story with multiple narrators all speaking at once. Not a collective "we," but a bunch of equal "I's." A multiple-first-person-narrator story, like Faulkner's *As I Lay Dying*, but with all the narrators talking at once.

And if one wanted to follow the metaphor out, perhaps to the breaking point, one might look at an ensemble performance led by someone like Duke Ellington or Jelly Roll Morton as a kind of third-person narrative, where an omniscient central narrator provides a highly orchestrated context for the actions and statements of the various "characters" as they arise.

You could even call jazz novelistic, in that we are afforded a look not just at the "external," dramatic interactions among the "characters" but, in a sense, at their inner thoughts as well. Or perhaps the dramatic situation of jazz more closely resembles that of Shakespearean drama, in which we get not only the external action and dialogue but also the revealing of inner thoughts through soliloquy.

Well, we don't need to follow the metaphor out all the way. It may be enough to say that these elements are present in jazz in their own ways. Jazz has a specifically dramatic component to it. The situation of a jazz group playing is dramatic by its very nature. It involves risk, the presentation of characters among whom there is both tension and harmony, and it provides for the resolution, or at least the playing out, of that tension. A jazz performance takes place over time, and hence involves at least an implicit philosophical stance regarding cause and effect, or the absence of same, and also the fact of an ending.

So jazz contains many of the essential elements of dramatic narrative. The degree to which performers can set up our expectations and then either satisfy or interestingly subvert them, creating suspense, pathos, joy, excitement, tenderness, humor, are very much at the center of our experience of a jazz performance. It is a bit of a paradox, because music, except for certain kinds of "program" music, doesn't refer to literal events beyond itself. Music may be conscripted into an opera or a film, or a composer may try to depict a storm or a river, but finally, if the music doesn't work on its own terms, no amount of narrative exoskeleton will save it from triviality, or pretentiousness, or worse. In music, the telling of the story is itself the dramatic action.

There is no one way to tell a story properly, and that is a large part of the point of jazz. If you just want to hear the story, the myth, repeated, without the personal element in the telling, what is it you really want? Maybe some sense of the absolute that can absolve you of the pain of being particular, specific, finite? The repetition of the same notions, in the same tone, over and over, is the stock-in-trade of any type of fundamentalist, for whom no deviation from The Text, whatever The Text happens to be, is allowed.

Integral to any concept of jazz, along with all the ordering elements, is that quasi-anarchic, unpredictable, never-satisfied personal element—the unrepeatable, the exception to the rule. It is integral to the music. It is an indispensable part of the picture, among all the other elements. Having something to say in any art means at least implicitly working out your own sense of the relation between the individualistic, unpredictable aspect of the self and the ordering, contextualizing, socialized part. Both parts need to be there.

Too often, in discourse, things get broken down into battles between contending opposites, with one implicitly needing to win out. But that either/or scheme doesn't accurately reflect anything about reality, which always has to do with the coexistence of opposites. It is the tension between unlike elements that gives reality its texture.

2

Just as a musician, or a person, who was all imagination and no knowledge would be seriously limited in his or her ability to relate to others and make meaningful statements, a person who was all knowledge and no imagination would have trouble holding our attention outside of a technical classroom. And even there . . .

All good artists are interested in means—in tools and technique. But one of the facts about art is that, while it can be appreciated and analyzed on a technical, intellectual level, it usually carries with it another meaning that hits us somewhere else. What that other meaning is, and where it hits us, can be as different and varied as the sensibilities of the artists, and of their listeners. But it's what makes art more than just a game. A musician can analyze Coleman Hawkins's great 1939 solo on "Body and Soul" and learn a lot about harmony, but one can also listen to the recording just to hear Hawkins tell his story, which has a way of moving us even if we don't have the equipment to analyze it.

If jazz is a set of tensions among opposites, then it shouldn't be a surprise to find that it also shows great tension between the intensely personal and the collaborative, or consensus, elements. But it is the individual use to which the consensus elements are put that makes things interesting.

This is the hardest aspect of jazz to discuss meaningfully; it resists being quantified or objectified. It is ultimately the most personal, since it deals with the most intimate, unrepeatable part of what it means to be an artist, with what the artist wants to express on a deep level. To come to grips with it entails an investment of the listener's own personal self, which is called out to meet the music's message halfway.

Years ago I visited the late tenor saxophonist Buddy Tate at his house on Long Island. Tate had played with the great wartime Count Basie band next to Lester Young, and was a veteran of decades playing for dancers and listeners in nightclubs and bars and hotels and jazz festivals. He was well over six feet tall, and he used to wear fantastic suits made of shiny material with embossed patterns on them, and he still, when I talked to him, was traveling all over the world. His sound on the tenor was so big that it inhabited your chest while he played. He wanted me to hear a recording he had made in the early 1960s with his old Basie bandmate trumpeter Buck Clayton.

I stood next to him in his living room in the late afternoon with the sun coming through the blinds—I was maybe twenty; Tate must have been in his fifties—listening to Buck Clayton's trumpet play the blues at the most relaxed tempo, and Buddy watched me as I listened, and he kind of raised one eyebrow. "Do you hear that, Tom?" I wasn't sure what it was he wanted me to hear. The phrases Clayton played were simple, conversational; they seemed to put things in a certain way, and then answer them; they sat against the chords the pianist was playing with a kind of bitter-sweetness. "He's telling a story," Tate said.

When it was over, he said, "He had something he wanted to say. Do you see?" It was almost thirty years ago, and I thought Buddy Tate would be around forever, and I was still thinking about what Buck Clayton had just played—it was over so quickly, and I was trying to hold on to it—and I thought what Buddy was saying to me was more or less self-evident. Of course Buck Clayton had something he wanted to say. But it wasn't really that simple.

Clayton's choruses had a bittersweet element that had to do with the fact of limitation and finitude itself. Whatever else that solo was about, it was also, in a way, his personal statement about the context itself—the song's form, the always beginning and ending and beginning again of the short blues choruses, the transient quality of sound and time itself. Things last only a short time, he seemed to be saying, but there is always a beginning again. There was nothing sentimental or maudlin in that recognition, and neither was there any bogus triumphalism. Buck and Buddy were looking things straight in the eye.

~~~

There are many ways of telling a story, as opposed to making random remarks. Of course, sometimes things that seem disconnected at first turn out later to have had a pattern all along. Stories don't have to be linear, or involve a climax and a denouement, or any of the other obvious "story" elements. But it is worth saying that any story that seems oblivious to the fact that it will not last forever, or say everything there is to say, won't be a very deep story. Any story needs to grasp its own finitude before it can say what it has to say. The same is true of a person. No one story, no one person—no society, for that matter—can say or do everything, even if we had unlimited time, which we don't. Given that fact, what do you want to say? How do you want to be in the world?

Every jazz musician, every artist, answers this question in his or her own way. It is that grasping of who they are, a truth that can't be put into words, that allows them to say what they have to say. Sonny Rollins and Stan Getz both play tenor saxophone, Dizzy Gillespie and Miles Davis both play trumpet, Duke Ellington and Count Basie both play piano, but no one could mistake one for the other. Each one finds a way to open a space for his own unique sense of being in the world. If they were repeatable units, most of us would not call them artists.

Someone could argue that one could have a very individuated sense of being but still express ugliness or evil. And it is true that the individual, as we know from Dostoevsky if from nowhere else, will often do horrible things just to prove to himself that he is still free. But I think experience bears out the notion that the truly individualized does not go in the direction of ugliness and evil. Brutality and evil tend to dehumanize, turn people into units, and either manipulate or destroy them. Art is, among other things, an action against the forces that tend to standardize and diminish the individual.

Once, at the Iowa Writers' Workshop, the great Mississippi writer Barry Hannah came to visit and conduct a two-day workshop in which he critiqued a handful of student stories. One of these stories had a lot of surface action, a lot of tonal poses, gestures in the direction of affect, but there was also a quality of randomness about it, and Hannah was trying to explain this to the students who were discussing it. One of the workshoppers, arguing with Hannah over his reading, said, "I like this because it has a lot of drive." And Barry, who was also, come to think of it, a trumpeter, squinted a little and leaned forward and said, "Yes, but what is it driving *at?*"

What is necessary? What lasts for you, and what falls away, and what is the relation between them? Where do you stand? What do you make of being human and limited and mortal? Ultimate questions, with no obvious or fixed answers. But asking them is still important.

Further Listening:
Telling a Story

What follows is my own list of some of my own favorite jazz stories and storytellers on record, things that have been necessary to me, that have lasted. It is not an attempt to make a canonical list for study, or to illustrate certain objective points; it is, rather, a sort of subjective anti-canon of only the things that have spoken to me most eloquently and personally over the years that I've been listening. Every jazz fan has a personal list, even if he or she has never bothered to write it down. So since this chapter has dealt mainly with the personal and the unquantifiable, this list answers to no larger point than my own sense of what has mattered most, for me. I hope you will make your own list.

~~~

Louis Armstrong was the first great storyteller in jazz, and it is pointless to start listing one's favorite Armstrong solos. But people rarely talk about his early solos with the Fletcher Henderson Orchestra, and I have always gotten a special kick out of hearing his crackling, swinging trumpet emerge out of some of those stiff early arrangements, especially on "Shanghai Shuffle," on the Henderson set *A Study in Frustration* (Columbia/Legacy). Another neglected beauty is "Alone at Last," on which he takes a lovely solo in a very straitlaced setting with the Henderson band playing under the name the Southern Serenaders, available on the essential box set

Louis Armstrong: Portrait of the Artist as a Young Man (Columbia/ Legacy). That set also contains the January 1925 version of "Cake Walking Babies from Home," recorded under Clarence Williams's leadership, on which Armstrong battles New Orleans soprano saxophone master Sidney Bechet to a thrilling climax. For that matter, *Portrait* also includes one of my favorite Louis big-band recordings, the 1930 "Ding Dong Daddy (from Dumas)," with that series of fabulous breaks toward the end; and "Too Busy," with the singer Lillie Delk Christian, on which Armstrong, pianist Earl Hines, and clarinetist Jimmie Noone each plays a brief solo in the middle of the record, and then Louis comes back and scats a vocal accompaniment to Christian's second vocal chorus; and the 1934 recording of "Song of the Vipers," one of Armstrong's most mysterious and beautiful recordings, and I know I said I wouldn't get started talking about Louis Armstrong solos, so that's it. Besides, *Portrait* isn't perfect. It doesn't, for example, contain the 1931 track "The Lonesome Road" (Columbia/Legacy), with Armstrong parodying a preacher, and its beautiful, simple, and poetic 16-bar Armstrong solo, or . . .

Cornetist Bix Beiderbecke was Armstrong's contemporary, and one of the music's true poets. His best solos were elegant and perfectly shaped, absolutely unmistakable as his own, and full of beauty. "Singing the Blues," with saxophonist Frank Trumbauer (Columbia/Legacy), contains probably the best single solo he recorded, and is one of the great jazz records overall. His solos on "Ostrich Walk" and "Riverboat Shuffle," also with Trumbauer, are marvels, so relaxed and focused, brief gems that breathe an entire world into existence. His solos with the big band of Paul Whiteman on tunes such as "Lonely Melody," "From Monday On," and "Changes" (RCA/BMG) rise out of the often heavy-footed Whiteman setting so eloquently, like Armstrong's solos with Fletcher Henderson, although the two men had very different sensibilities.

Records from jazz's early decades were short, because of the limited time available on the 78-rpm records of that time, and often very brief solo statements stand out in memory out of all proportion to the clock time they take up. The little-known cornetist Ward Pinkett's solo on Jelly Roll Morton's 1928 "Georgia Swing" (RCA/BMG), for example, which is so short (16 bars) and swings so much and makes so much sense. Or the short-lived Chicago clarinetist Frank Teschemacher's solos and ensemble playing on "Friars' Point Shuffle" and "Darktown Strutters' Ball" with the Jungle Kings, and "Nobody's Sweetheart" with Charles Pierce and his Orchestra (originally recorded for Paramount in 1928, and reissued on imported labels), or his solos on "There'll Be Some Changes Made" and "I Found a New Baby" with the Chicago Rhythm Kings (Brunswick originally, available on imported labels). Or the great New Orleans trumpeter Red Allen's solo on his own 1929 recording of the blues "Feelin' Drowsy" (RCA/BMG), or trumpeter Irving "Mouse" Randolph's way of phrasing just the eight-bar bridge on Billie Holiday's 1936 "The Way You Look Tonight" with Teddy Wilson's band (Columbia/Legacy), or Frankie Newton's trumpet obbligato to Clarence Palmer's vocal on Newton's 1937 recording of "You Showed Me the Way" (Columbia/Legacy).

But nobody made more use of short solo space than tenor saxophonist Lester "Pres" Young, one of the greatest storytellers in jazz history. Eight bars from Lester Young could often say more, *mean* more, than hours of playing from some musicians, especially in his late-1930s recordings, when he was at his best, before years of drinking and hard living began to take their toll. His recorded solos with Count Basie's band often contained improvised phrases that stated things so exactly, with such originality and freshness and logic, that musicians quoted them for years to come. Basie records like "Jive at Five," "One O'Clock Jump," "Time Out," "Doggin' Around," "Every Tub," "Texas Shuffle" (on which Young plays clarinet), "Honeysuckle Rose," "You Can Depend on Me," "Roseland Shuffle," "Shorty George" (all Decca), "Taxi War Dance," "Miss Thing," "Twelfth Street Rag," "Pound Cake," "Riff Interlude," "I Never Knew," "Tickle Toe," "Louisiana," "Song of the Islands," "Blow Top," "Broadway," and "Easy Does It" (all Columbia/Legacy) all contain supremely beautiful, classic solos by Pres.

With Billie Holiday in the late 1930s, Pres also recorded many great solos, of which I wouldn't want to have to do without those on "I Must Have That Man," "When You're Smiling," "Mean to Me," "He Ain't Got Rhythm," and "Back in Your Own Backyard"; his melody statements on "Foolin' Myself," "This Year's Kisses," and "Easy Living"; and his unbelievable dialogue with Holiday in the last chorus of take 1 of "Me, Myself, and I" (all Columbia/ Legacy). And I always revisit his solos on the small-group performances "Lady Be Good" and "Shoe Shine Boy" with Jones-Smith Incorporated (Columbia/Legacy), "Countless Blues," "Pagin' the Devil," "Way Down Yonder in New Orleans," and especially "Them There Eyes" with the Kansas City Six (Commodore), "Basie English" with Johnny Guarnieri (Savoy), the 1943 recordings of "Just You, Just Me," "I Never Knew," and "Sometimes I'm Happy" (Keynote), and "I Never Knew," "Wholly Cats," and "Charlie's Dream" from a 1940 session with Benny Goodman and Charlie Christian, included on the four-disc Christian set *The Genius of the Electric Guitar* (Columbia/Legacy).

Billie Holiday also seemed to hit a vein of special magic when she recorded with trumpeter Roy Eldridge, and her early recordings of otherwise inconsequential pop songs, such as "It's Too Hot for Words," "What a Night, What a Moon, What a Boy," "Yankee Doodle Never Went to Town," and "Twenty-Four Hours a Day" (Columbia/Legacy), have a great freshness and joy, not just during her vocals but also in the exultant Eldridge-led out choruses. And it is impossible to get tired of hearing both takes of Eldridge's own 1937 "Wabash Stomp" (Columbia/Legacy).

Everyone knows that everyone needs to hear Coleman Hawkins's classic 1939 recording of "Body and Soul" (RCA/BMG), but lesser-known items such as the intense blues "Sih-Sah" (Vogue) and the unaccompanied solo "Picasso" (Verve) are equally profound. Hawkins's solo on take 2 of Fletcher Henderson's 1934 "Hocus Pocus" (RCA/BMG) is one of my favorite moments, as is his go-for-broke two-chorus solo on "Crazy Rhythm," recorded in Paris with a band including the Gypsy guitarist Django Reinhardt and altoist Benny Carter. Django was also present for one of the greatest jazz conversations ever recorded, between trombonist Dicky Wells and trumpeter Bill Coleman on "Sweet Sue, Just You" (Swing/DRG); the level of invention and wit in their four-bar exchanges is something to behold. Django Reinhardt always had something beautiful and poetic to say in his 1930s recordings with the Quintet of the Hot Club of France (various import labels), on which he was paired with violinist Stephane Grappelli. But I also love Django's unaccompanied solo recordings, such as "Parfum," "Echoes of Spain," "Improvisation," numbers 1 and 2, and others (again, import labels).

Ben Webster's solos with the Duke Ellington Orchestra in the early 1940s are justly famous (I especially love his solo on "St.

Louis Blues," recorded live in Fargo, North Dakota, in 1940 and released on Vintage Jazz Classics), but some of my favorite Webster is on the mid-1950s recordings he made with piano genius Art Tatum and currently available as part of the *Tatum Group Masterpieces* (Pablo); ballads such as "My One and Only Love," "Have You Met Miss Jones?," and "My Ideal" have an exquisite combination of strength and tenderness, and a real mood, as does Webster's playing on the album *The Warm Moods*, with strings arranged by Johnny Richards (Discovery). Webster's friend Budd Johnson was one of the undersung heroes of jazz, with a career covering more than five decades. His unique sound and inventiveness on both tenor and soprano saxophone always astound me, especially on three tracks—"Sometimes I'm Happy," "Red River Remembered," and "Moten Swing"—on *Earl Hines Live at the Village Vanguard* (Columbia/Legacy). And the exchanges between tenors Buddy Tate and Illinois Jacquet on "Sunday," from *Buddy Tate and his Buddies* (Chiaroscuro), are endlessly enjoyable.

For some reason, the song "I'll Remember April" has brought out some of my favorite playing. Bud Powell's solo on a live 1950 version from Birdland with Charlie Parker and Fats Navarro (various import labels) conveys such intelligence and exhilaration (Powell's solo on " 'Round Midnight," from the same set, is another of the great solos). The version by trumpeter Red Rodney with altoist Charles McPherson, pianist Barry Harris, bassist Sam Jones, and drummer Roy Brooks on the disc *Bird Lives!* (Muse) is fantastic, as is a live recording by Parker himself from a Boston-area club called Christy's, on the disc *The Happy Bird* (Parker). I first heard the Parker version in a farmers' market on Long Island when I was maybe twelve years old; the proprietor of the record booth played it for me, and as Bird's alto came out of the speakers, a man neither of us knew stopped in his tracks and said, "Is that Charlie Parker?" And then there's the alto solo by the little-known Dave Schildkraut, on Miles Davis's 1954 version (Prestige).

Charlie Parker's many classic solos have been written about and discussed at great length. Two that don't necessarily have that much historical significance but that are favorite moments of mine are his informal, idea-laden improvisation on "Cherokee" titled "Warming Up a Riff" (Savoy); and his entrance on the 1949 live performance of "The Closer," with Jazz at the Philharmonic (Verve); after a nearly hysterical climactic solo by Roy Eldridge, the tune ends, there is wild applause, then drummer Buddy Rich starts up the tempo again, by himself, the audience quiets down a little, and Bird comes in wailing. It actually isn't one of his best solos, but the moment is so great. And the entire 1951 live set *Bird at St. Nick's* (Fantasy), horrible sound quality and all, has some of the most inspired Bird there is to hear. Singer Eddie Jefferson's "Birdland Story," recorded with saxophonist James Moody (Chess), tells a story of seeing Charlie Parker, Dizzy Gillespie, Bud Powell, and a gang of other bebop giants at the famous New York nightclub, and is a lot of fun. And why leave out the exchanges between trumpeters Fats Navarro and Howard McGhee on "Double Talk" (Blue Note)?

Saxophonist Jimmy Heath, once nicknamed "Little Bird," usually has something interesting to say; I always go back to his solo on "Ray's Idea," with Miles Davis (Blue Note), and his playing on *Hub Cap* with Freddie Hubbard (Blue Note). Tenor saxophonist Brew Moore is sadly underrecognized, almost unknown today, but at his best, he was one of the music's poets. His album *Brew Moore* (Fantasy) contains some of the most relaxed tenor playing you'll ever hear, and his ballad performance of "Nancy with the Laughing Face" is gentle and warm and heartbreakingly poignant.

Miles Davis's lyricism is so well known by now that it needs no recommendation from me, but a performance that I need to hear periodically is his great and mysterious "Smooch" (Prestige), with Charles Mingus on piano. Wayne Shorter's tenor solo on "Fall," from Davis's *Nefertiti* (Columbia/Legacy), and Sonny Rollins's solo on Davis's 1953 "In Your Own Sweet Way" (Prestige), are also breathtaking, lyrical, and inventive statements, as is Tommy Flanagan's brief piano solo on this latter tune.

Flanagan is always eloquent; his solos always sparkle. My favorite is probably his solo on Wes Montgomery's recording of "D-Natural Blues," from *Incredible Jazz Guitar* (Riverside). Pianist Cedar Walton is also a brilliant and witty melodist, even at biting tempos; his solos on "Dingbat Blues," from trumpeter Blue Mitchell's album *The Cup Bearers* (Riverside), and throughout Freddie Hubbard's disc *Hub Cap* (Blue Note) fizz with intelligence and spontaneity.

And then there are Clifford Brown's trumpet solos on his own recording of "Hymn of the Orient" (Blue Note), and also on "Split Kick" and "Wee Dot" from Art Blakey's *A Night at Birdland*, volumes 1 and 2 (Blue Note); they never, ever wear out, no matter how many times I hear them. Nor does tenor saxophonist Dexter Gordon's solo on "The Panther" (Prestige), or his nine-and-a-half-minute odyssey on "Dexter's Deck," from Booker Ervin's album *Settin' the Pace* (Prestige), on which the rhythm section, with pianist Jaki Byard at the helm, provides a kaleidoscopically varied accompaniment. There's baritone saxophonist Serge Chaloff's whole quartet album *Blue Serge* (Capitol), and Lee Konitz's *Figure and Spirit* (Progressive), and Cannonball Adderley's *Something Else* (Blue Note), as well as Adderley's supreme solo on "Love for Sale" with Miles Davis (Columbia/Legacy).

And Charles McPherson's amazing alto solo on "Orange Was the Color of Her Dress, Then Blue Silk," off *Mingus at Monterey* (Prestige); and Sonny Rollins's "Skylark," from his *Next Album* (Milestone); Thelonious Monk's ingenious solo on "Straight No Chaser," from the album of the same title (Columbia/Legacy), on which his playing gets simpler and simpler with each chorus until it finally evaporates; and the haunting mood in Monk's playing throughout the solo album *Thelonious Alone in San Francisco* (Riverside); and also his recording of "Hackensack" (Prestige), with the great solos by tenorist Frank Foster and trumpeter Ray Copeland, under which Monk's accompaniment is so flexible and brilliant.

And I can't leave out Hank Mobley's smoky and propulsive version of "Hello, Young Lovers," from *Another Workout* (Blue Note), which generates such excitement, and is a great track even though the group has sped up unconscionably by the end of it—surprising with Wynton Kelly, Paul Chambers, and Philly Joe Jones involved, but everybody makes mistakes, I guess.

And where would I start with John Coltrane? Probably with "Wise One" and "Crescent" and "Bessie's Blues" from his album *Crescent*, and the entire albums *Ballads* and *John Coltrane and Johnny Hartman* (all Impulse). But then there are also all those great Atlantic tracks, not just the obvious ones but "The Night Has a Thousand Eyes" and "Liberia" and "My Shining Hour" . . . And I always revisit the surprise of hearing Ornette Coleman's alto audaciously reinventing the blues on "Ramblin'," from *Change of the Century* (Atlantic), but also his amazing trio tracks such as "Faces and Places" and "Dee Dee" on *At the Golden Circle*, volume 1 (Blue Note), or, even better, "Doughnut" from *Town Hall, 1962* (ESP) . . .

∿∿∿

. . . and I know I'm forgetting some. I haven't even mentioned Oscar Pettiford, or Bud Freeman's great recording of "The Eel," or the Art Tatum set *Twentieth Century Piano Genius* (Verve), or Earl Hines's *Quintessential Continued* (Chiaroscuro). There is no way to say it all, and no matter how much you say, you can only begin to suggest the immensity and richness of the landscape. So I will wrap up this solo for now, only for now.

Acknowledgments

This book is dedicated . . .

. . . with thanks to Mom, who supported my interest in music long before I could support it myself,

. . . to the memory of my father, who always wanted to understand everything. He loved jazz, and he didn't understand it, and it frustrated him. I hope he would have liked this book,

. . . to Dan Morgenstern, who loves jazz and has spent his life writing about it better than anyone, and to Professor Emeritus David Park of Williams College, who encouraged some of my early forays into territory covered by this book,

. . . to all the jazz musicians who have made time and space for me in their lives, and especially in memory of Milt Hinton, Tommy Flanagan, Dicky Wells, Buddy Tate, Rudy Powell, Jaki Byard, Budd Johnson, Jo Jones, Mary Lou Williams, Eddie Jefferson, Clifford Jordan, and Sanford Gold,

. . . to Wynton Marsalis, Stanley Crouch, and Albert Murray, who have had the courage of their convictions and have achieved so much, at Jazz at Lincoln Center and beyond,

. . . and with so much love and gratitude—such inadequate words—to Mary Howell, my better half by far.

It comes with thanks, as well, to Jazz at Lincoln Center's Laura Johnson, who wanted me to write this and kept after me until I agreed, and to Kate Medina and Robin Rolewicz at Random House, who have been great to work with.

Special thanks to my agent, Amy Williams—patient, generous, loyal, and wise—without whom this book would truly not have been possible, to Joe DeSalvo for his generosity and friendship, and to Dave Rodriguez, who helped keep the gears running.

CD Track Information

1. **"Weather Bird Rag"/King Oliver's Creole Jazz Band** (used courtesy of Concord Music Group; publisher: Louis Armstrong Music c/o Music Sales Corp., ASCAP; composer: Louis Armstrong)

   King Oliver's Creole Jazz Band: Joe "King" Oliver and Louis Armstrong (cornets), Honore Dutrey (trombone), Johnny Dodds (clarinet), Lillian Hardin (piano), Bill Johnson (banjo), Warren "Baby" Dodds (drums).

   Recorded in Richmond, Indiana, April 6, 1923. Matrix no. 11388. Originally issued on Gennet 5132. Transferred from CD: Retrieval RTR 79007 (King Oliver's Creole Jazz Band/*The Complete Set*).

2. **"Boogie Woogie (I May Be Wrong)"/Count Basie and Lester Young** (used courtesy of Sony BMG; publisher: Bregman Vocco & Conn, Inc., c/o WB Music Corp./Warner Chappell Music, Inc., ASCAP; composer: Count Basie/James Andrew Rushing)

   Jones-Smith Incorporated: Carl "Tatti" Smith (trumpet), Lester Young (tenor sax), Count Basie (piano), Walter Page (bass), Jo Jones (drums), Jimmy Rushing (vocal).

   Recorded in Chicago, Illinois, November 9, 1936. Matrix no. C-1659-1. Originally issued on Vocalion 3459. Transferred from CD: Columbia C4K 87110 (Count Basie and His Orchestra/*America's No. 1 Band!: The Columbia Years*).

3. **"U.M.M.G. (Upper Manhattan Medical Group)"/Duke Ellington with Dizzy Gillespie** (used courtesy of Sony BMG.; publisher: Tempo Music, Inc., c/o Music Sales Corp., ASCAP; composer: Billy Strayhorn)

Duke Ellington and His Orchestra: Clark Terry, Harold "Shorty" Baker, Andres Ford, Ray Nance, and Dizzy Gillespie (trumpets); Britt Woodman, Quentin "Butter" Jackson, and John Sanders (trombones); Russell Procope and Johnny Hodges (alto saxophones); Jimmy Hamilton and Paul Gonsalves (tenor saxophones); Harry Carney (baritone saxophone); Duke Ellington (piano); Jimmy Woode (bass); Sam Woodyard (drums).

Recorded in New York, New York, February 19, 1959. Matrix no. CO 62195. Originally issued on Columbia CL 1323. Transferred from CD: Columbia CK 40712 (Duke Ellington/*Jazz Party*).

4. **"Moritat"/Sonny Rollins** (used courtesy of Concord Music Group; publisher: Kurt Weill Foundation/Music, Inc., c/o WB Music Corp/Warner Chappell Music, Inc., and Weill Brecht Harms Company, Inc., c/o Warner Bros., Inc., ASCAP; composer: Marc Blitzstein, Eugen Berthold Brecht, Kurt Weill)

Sonny Rollins Quartet: Sonny Rollins (tenor saxophone), Tommy Flanagan (piano), Doug Watkins (bass), Max Roach (drums).

Recorded in Hackensack, New Jersey, June 22, 1956. Matrix no. 922. Originally issued on Prestige 7079. Transferred from CD: Prestige PRCD-7079-2 (Sonny Rollins/*Saxophone Colossus*).

5. **"I Can't Get Started"/Stan Getz** (used courtesy of Universal Music Enterprises; publisher: Chappell & Co, Inc., c/o Warner Chappell Music, Inc., and Ira Gershwin Music c/o WB Music Corp. and WB Music Corp c/o Warner Bros., Inc., ASCAP; composer: Duke Vernon/Ira Gershwin)

Stan Getz (tenor saxophone), Kenny Barron (piano), Rufus Reid (bass), Victor Lewis (drums).

Recorded live at the Montmartre Club in Copenhagen, July 6, 1987. Transferred from CD: EmArcy 838 769-2 (Stan Getz/*Anniversary*).

6. **"Footprints"/Miles Davis Quintet** (used courtesy of Sony BMG; publisher: Irving Music, Inc./Wayne Shorter, Inc., c/o Miyako Music, BMI; composer: Wayne Shorter)

   Miles Davis Quintet: Miles Davis (trumpet), Wayne Shorter (tenor saxophone), Herbie Hancock (piano), Ron Carter (bass), Tony Williams (drums).

   Recorded in New York, New York, October 25, 1966. Matrix no. CO 91178-4. Originally issued on Columbia CS 9401/CL2601. Transferred from CD: Columbia C6K67398 (*Miles Davis Quintet 1965–68*).

7. **"The Eternal Triangle"/Dizzy Gillespie, Sonny Rollins, Sonny Stitt** (used courtesy of Universal Music Enterprises; publisher: Second Floor Music c/o R&H Music, BMI; composer: Sonny Edward Stitt)

   Dizzy Gillespie (trumpet), Sonny Rollins and Sonny Stitt (tenor saxophones), Ray Bryant (piano), Tommy Bryant (bass), Charlie Persip (drums).

   Recorded in New York, New York, December 19, 1957. Originally issued on Verve MGV 8262. Transferred from CD: Verve 314 521 426-2 (Dizzy Gillespie–Sonny Rollins–Sonny Stitt/*Sonny Side Up*).

Billie Holiday at a New York jam session, 1939. Back row, from left: Bud Freeman, tenor saxophone; J. C. Higginbotham, trombone; Harry Lim, record producer; Eddie Condon, guitar; Clyde Newcomb, bass. Front row, from left: Dave Bowman, piano; Billie Holiday, vocalist; Ernie Anderson, promoter; unidentified trumpet player; Max Kaminsky, drums. Photograph by Charles Peterson, courtesy of Don Peterson.

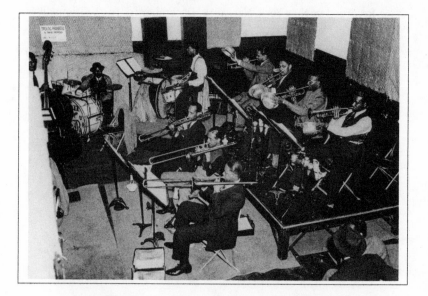

Brass section of the Count Basie Orchestra at a Columbia recording session in New York City, 1940. Photograph courtesy of the Frank Driggs Collection.

Index

Page numbers in italics indicate photographs.

126–28; listening suggestions, 120–26; "Moritat" example, 106; and popular songs, 106–7

Harris, Barry, 181

Harris, Bill, 36

Harrison, Jimmy, 30

Hawkins, Coleman: and "Ah-Leu-Cha," 28; and bebop, 36; and blues form, 48, 68, 72, 73; and "Body and Soul," 90, 122, 171, 180; and Coltrane, 43; and Fletcher Henderson, 30, 180; and Hampton, 33; and Monk, 40; and Pettiford, 37; as storyteller, 180; and swing, 155, 159

Hawkins, Erskine, 67

Haynes, Roy, 73

Heath, Jimmy, 182

Heath, Percy, 39, 158

Henderson, Fletcher: about, 29–30; and Armstrong, 9, 176–77; as composer/arranger, 10, 91; as nurturer of star soloists, 29–30; and swing, 154

Henderson, Horace, 29, 91

Henderson, Joe, 45

Hendrix, Jimi, 58

Henry, Ernie, 40

Herman, Woody, 36, 48, 155

Higgins, Billy, 29, 44, 119, 128

Hill, Andrew, 45

Hines, Earl: and Armstrong, 177; and boogie-woogie, 67; as storyteller, 185; and "Weather Bird," 26, 88–89

Hodges, Johnny, 31, 33, 34, 43, 68

Holiday, Billie: and blues form, 73; and "Body and Soul," 122; and improvisation, 120–21; as storyteller, 180; and swing, 132; and Wilson, 33, 90, 178; and Young, 179

Hot Five and Hot Seven recordings, 9, 25, 62

House, Son, 61, 62

Hubbard, Freddie, 29, 158, 182, 183

"I Can't Get Started" (track 5): about, 190; compared with "Moritat," 15–16; compared with "Weather Bird Rag," 149; and Getz, 4, 15–16, 57, 82; instrumental vocal effects, 57; and passage of time, 149; relationship between background and foreground, 4; rhythmic effects, 139; telling the story, 168; variation on song form, 82

improvisation: about, 4–5, 103–5; basic role of rhythm section, 11; and "Boogie Woogie," 11–12; and chord progressions, 108, 109, 110–11; defined, 103–4; and "The Eternal Triangle," 21–22, 111, 112, 113–16; extended length, 13, 99; and "Footprints," 113, 117–18; group, 7–8, 9, 25–29, 42–45, 100–101; and harmonic structure, 105, 106–7; listening suggestions, 120–29; and melodic imagination, 105, 112–16, 118; modal approach, 117–18, 126–28; in New Orleans jazz, 8–9, 25–27; role of chorus-based form, 105–6; same song by different musicians, 121–23; same song by same musician but different versions, 123–25

Izenzon, David, 44, 129

Jackson, Mahalia, 94

Jackson, Milt, 39, 70, 71

Jacquet, Illinois, 155, 159, 181

jam sessions, 13, 21

James, Harry, 10, 32

James, Skip, 61, 62

jazz: 1960s avant-garde, 28–29, 42–45; and blues form, 47, 48–49, 57, 66; individual differences among players, 121–23, 174; orchestrating for larger ensembles, 10, 12, 18–21, 29–32, 84–86; and popular song form, 76–82; relationship between background and foreground, 3–5, 11–13; as social situation, 3; as storytelling, 168–75; tensions in, 4, 53, 84, 131–32; theatrical element, 14; *see also* improvisation; New Orleans jazz

Jazz Messengers, *see* Blakey, Art

Jefferson, Blind Lemon, 61, 62

Jefferson, Eddie, 122, 182

Jobim, Antonio Carlos, 145, 162

Johnson, Bill, 130

Johnson, Budd, 181

Johnson, J. J., 70, 98, 158

Johnson, Pete, 67

Johnson, Robert, 62

Jones, Elvin, 17, 43, 148, 164

Jones, Jo, 12, 49

rhythm section: basic role in improvisation, 11; defined, 11; and "The Eternal Triangle," 21, 138; and "Footprints," 11, 17–18, 51; relationship to soloist, 11–13, 17

Rich, Buddy, 182

Richards, Johnny, 181

Richmond, Dannie, 27, 38, 159

riffs: and bebop, 34; in "Boogie Woogie," 11–12; defined, 11; in "The Eternal Triangle," 22

Rivers, Sam, 164

Roach, Max: and bebop, 36; and blues form, 66; and Monk, 40; and "Moritat," 14, 15, 57, 81; and musical forms, 99; and swing, 157; and waltz tempo, 162–63

rock and roll, 58, 131

Rodgers, Jimmie, 57

Rodney, Red, 181

Rollins, Sonny: and blues form, 70, 71; and "Body and Soul," 122; and calypso music, 125–26, 161; and "The Eternal Triangle," 21, 22, 78–79, 138–39; and "Freedom Suite," 99; and improvisation, 125–26; and Monk, 40; and "Moritat," 4, 12–13, 14, 15, 56–57, 80, 81, 106; and musical forms, 99; photo, 102; pianoless band, 40; and Powell, 35; recasting of familiar tunes, 125; and Stitt, 113–16; as storyteller, 183, 184; and swing, 158, 159; and waltz tempo, 163

Rouse, Charlie, 41

Rushing, Jimmy, 12, 46, 49, 50, 52, 58, 135

Russell, George, 20, 39, 92, 98

Sauter, Eddie, 39, 92

Schuller, Gunther, 98

Scorsese, Martin, 61

Scott, James, 87

Shakespeare, 169

"shave and a haircut" bar pattern, 144–45

"sheets of sound," 127

Sherman, James, 121

Shorter, Wayne: and Davis, 41, 99–100, 148, 164; and "Footprints," 17, 51–52, 99; photo, 2; as storyteller, 183

Shostakovich, Dmitri, 56

Silver, Horace, 41, 70, 72, 158

Sims, Zoot, 36, 71, 155

Smith, Bessie, 63, 136

Smith, Carl, 11, 12, 49, 56

Smith, Clara, 63

Smith, Jabbo, 10

Smith, Jimmy, 72

Smith, Joe, 10, 30

Smith, Mamie, 48

Smith, Stuff, 156

Smith, Trixie, 63

songs, see blues; popular songs

Spanier, Muggsy, 10, 27, 64

Spanish tinge: defined, 142; listening suggestions, 159–62; simple, 142–43; variants, 143–44; "Weather Bird Rag" example, 143

Stark, Bobby, 30

Stewart, Rex, 10, 30, 31, 34, 66

Stitt, Sonny: and Coltrane, 43; and "The Eternal Triangle," 21, 22, 54–55, 78, 79, 112, 138; and Rollins, 113–16; and swing, 158

storytelling, 168–75

Strayhorn, Billy: as composer/arranger, 18, 19, 20, 31, 95; and "U.M.M.G.," 18, 19, 83, 85

Sun Ra, 165

swing era: defined, 12; influence of New Orleans jazz on, 27–28; see also big bands

swinging, 132–35, 136, 138, 139–40, 146, 147, 153–62

Tate, Buddy, 172–73, 181

Tatum, Art, 48, 123, 181

Taylor, Cecil, 44

Tchaikovsky, Piotr 95

Teagarden, Charlie, 10

Teagarden, Jack, 30, 48, 64

tempo, see time

Terry, Clark, 35, 74, 121

Teschemacher, Frank, 64, 178

"third-stream" music, 98–99

Thompson, Lucky, 70, 158

Thornhill, Claude, 36

time: "The Eternal Triangle" example, 134; "Footprints" example, 134–35; 4/4 time, 140–47; playing with, 134, 147–48, 163–65; sense of passing, 148–52; see also phrasing; rhythm

Time Out, 39, 99

Tizol, Juan, 74
Tjader, Cal, 161
trading eights, 15
trading fours, 15
Trumbauer, Frank, 30, 96, 159, 177
Turner, Joe, 67, 156
Turrentine, Stanley, 72
Tyner, McCoy, 43, 148, 164

"U.M.M.G." (track 3): about, 189; and
    chord changes, 111; compared with
    "Weather Bird Rag," 149; and
    Ellington, 4, 18–20, 83; and Gilles-
    pie, 4, 19, 83, 85, 86; influence of
    composer-arranger, 18–20, 85–86,
    94; and passage of time, 149; per-
    formance arc, 76, 83–84; relation-
    ship between background and
    foreground, 4, 18–19; trombone
    mute example, 56
upbeat, defined, 141, 146

Venuti, Joe, 64
vocals: blues singers with jazz accompa-
    niment, 63; and improvisation,
    120–21; instrumental effects,
    56–57; Rushing on "Boogie Woo-
    gie" track, 12, 49, 50, 52, 58, 135;
    see also Holiday, Billie

Wallace, Sippie, 63
Waller, Fats, 33, 48, 155–56
Walton, Cedar, 183
Washington, Dinah, 121
Waters, Muddy, 61
Watkins, Doug, 15, 81
"Weather Bird," 26, 88–89
"Weather Bird Rag" (track 1): about,
    189; and Armstrong, 6, 8–9, 88;
    breaks in, 8–9; compared with "I
    Can't Get Started," 149; compared

with "U.M.M.G.", 149; compared
    with "Weather Bird," 26; descrip-
    tion of structure, 88; as example of
    ragtime music, 88–89; group sto-
    rytelling, 168–69; instrumental
    vocal effects, 56; and Oliver, 5–6,
    8–9, 24, 56, 88; and passage of
    time, 149; performance length, 83;
    relationship between background
    and foreground, 5, 8–9; Spanish-
    tinge rhythm in, 143
Webster, Ben: and blues form, 66, 68,
    71–72, 73; and Ellington, 31, 66,
    180–81; and Fletcher Henderson,
    30; and Hampton, 33; as storyteller,
    180–81; and swing, 154, 158, 159
Weill, Kurt, see "Moritat" (track 4)
Wells, Dicky, 180
Whiteman, Paul, 10, 30, 91, 96, 177
Williams, Clarence, 27, 177
Williams, Cootie, 10, 31, 33, 65
Williams, Hank, 58
Williams, Martin, 158
Williams, Mary Lou, 36, 48, 67, 92
Williams, Tony: and Davis, 41, 99–100,
    148, 163; and "Footprints," 11, 17,
    51, 99; photo, 2; playing with time,
    163–64
Williamson, Sonny Boy, 61
Wilson, Teddy, 32, 33, 90, 120, 156, 178
Woods, Jimmie, 111
Woodyard, Sam, 19

Young, Lester: and Basie, 32, 179; and
    blues form, 48, 65, 68, 73; and
    "Boogie Woogie," 11, 12, 49, 50; as
    clarinetist, 28, 65; and Holiday,
    120, 121, 179; and Kansas City Six,
    28, 65, 90, 159; photo, 46; as sto-
    ryteller, 178–79; and swing,
    158–59

About the Author

TOM PIAZZA is the author of seven books, including *The Guide to Classic Recorded Jazz*, which won an ASCAP–Deems Taylor Award, and the widely acclaimed novel *My Cold War*. A graduate of the Iowa Writers' Workshop, he has written for *The New York Times*, *The Atlantic Monthly*, *The Oxford American*, and many other publications. He is the recipient of a James Michener Fellowship in Fiction, and a 2004 Grammy Award for his album notes to *Martin Scorsese Presents the Blues: A Musical Journey*. He may be visited at www.tompiazza.com.

WYNTON MARSALIS is the artistic director of Jazz at Lincoln Center. Marsalis has won nine Grammy awards, and his oratorio on slavery and freedom, *Blood on the Fields*, is the first and, to date, only jazz composition to win the Pulitzer Prize in music.

JAZZ AT LINCOLN CENTER is a not-for-profit arts organization in New York City dedicated to jazz. Its education division reaches hundreds of thousands of students and educators as well as the general public annually through concerts, classes, workshops, and publications. www.jalc.org.